H.J. (Hugh) Westheuser
#1177 Bazett Rd.
Kelowna, B.C. V1Z 2T4
(604) 769-6605

TATSHENSHINI
Wilderness Quest
AND OTHER RIVER ADVENTURES

Canadian Cataloguing in Publication Data
Madsen, Ken, 1950-
  Tatshenshini wilderness quest and other river
adventure stories

  ISBN 1--89123-22--4

  1. Kayaking--Yukon Territory. 2. Kayaking--Alaska.
3. Canoes and canoeing--Yukon Territory. 4. Canoes
and canoeing--Alaska. 5. Rafting (Sports)--Yukon
Territory. 6. Rafting (Sports)--Alaska. 7. Wild and
scenic rivers-- Yukon Territory. 8. Wild and scenic
rivers Alaska. 9. Yukon Territory--Description and
travel--1981- 10. Alaska--Description and travel
--1981- 11. Wildlife conservation--Yukon Territory.
12. Wildlife conservation--Alaska. I. Western Canada
Wilderness Committee. II. Title.
GV776.15. Y8M32 1991   917.19'1   C91-091700-0

TATSHENSHINI
Wilderness Quest
AND OTHER RIVER ADVENTURES

KEN MADSEN

TATSHENSHINI WILDERNESS QUEST

AND OTHER RIVER ADVENTURES

Copyright © 1991 by Ken Madsen
All Rights Reserved
ISBN 1-895123-22-4

Published by Western Canada Wilderness Committee
and Primrose Publishing

Maps by Nola Johnston
Edited by Elaine Jones
Design consulting by Sue Fox
Printed by Hignell Printing

Thanks to the B.C. Archives and Records Service for "The Trail of '98 by the All Canadian Route," by Corp, Ernest J. (Call Number E-E-C81)

Photo Credits:
Wendy Boothroyd (pages 79, 85, 86, 90, 93, 109, 114, 129, 131, 133, 149, 151, 155, 157, and 159)
Public Archives of Canada (pages 82 and 99)
Yukon Archives (page 76)
All other photos by Ken Madsen

Cover Photo: Jody Schick on Alsek Lake
Back Cover Photo: Poco Bartels on the Alsek River
Page 2: Icebergs and Mt. Fairweather
Page 5: Turnback Canyon
Page 8: Icebergs in Alsek Lake
Page 12: Kirsten Madsen near the Tatshenshini
Page 14: Rapid below Turnback Canyon
Page 36: Walker Glacier
Page 60: Bald eagle by the Chilkat River
Page 76: Yukon River during the gold rush
Page 100: Firth River canyon
Page 124: Coal River canyon
Page 144: Snake River

Printed in Canada on recycled paper

ACKNOWLEDGEMENTS

Thanks to everyone who struggles to preserve wilderness areas. The following people helped with the Tatshenshini Wilderness Quest or with the preparation of this book.

Tatshenshini Wilderness Quest paddlers:
Derek Endress, Ian Pineau, and Jody Schick...three who help keep me young.

Jim Boothroyd
Sa Boothroyd
Wendy Boothroyd
Lauren Crooks
Ric Careless — Tatshenshini Wild
Peter Enticknapp — Lynn Canal Conservation, Inc.
Paul George — Western Canada Wilderness Committee
Monte Hummel — World Wildlife Fund
Bob Jickling
Sue Johnson
Kevin Kavanagh — World Wildlife Fund
Hector Mackenzie
Katy Madsen
Kirsten Madsen
Polly Madsen
Mailynne Ouellet
E. Robert Ross
Jack Schick
Joanne Schick
Rachel Shephard
Kate Williams

Arctic Edge
Canadian River Expeditions
Coast Mountain Sports
Harvest Food Works
Medicine Chest Pharmacy
Northern Outdoors
Predator Performance Designs

Thanks to Lotteries Yukon for an "Advanced Artist Development Grant" which helped to make this writing project possible.

CONTENTS

Foreword	....	10
Map of the Rivers	....	11
Tatshenshini Quest Map	....	13
No Risk of Boredom	Alsek River	15
Tatshenshini Wilderness Quest	Tatshenshini River	37
A Taste of Small-Town Politics	Chilkat River	61
One Century Apart	Hess River	77
Of Caribou and Oil	Firth River	101
Sand in My Surprise Peas	Coal River	125
Otters at $19.00	Snake River	145

FOREWORD

I never met the late Bill Mason, but like many Canadians, my life was touched by his.

After I became hooked on canoeing, I read and re-read his book, *The Path of the Paddle*, hoping to learn to run whitewater with some semblance of control. At first, all I wanted was to keep my canoe upright, but I soon realized that, like Bill Mason, I couldn't divorce the mechanics of paddling from a love of wilderness.

In *The Path of the Paddle*, Mason pretended that he had to choose between St. Paul's Cathedral and a waterfall hidden up a river that spills into Lake Superior. He chose the waterfall. While awe-struck by humanity's great artistic creations, he knew that they couldn't compete with the natural world.

When I taught a dozen grade ones and twos in a tiny village five hundred kilometres north of Whitehorse, my class and I followed the mythical journey of a tiny, hand-carved canoe in Mason's film, *Paddle to the Sea*. Several years later, my grade five students in Whitehorse, usually rebounding off the walls, sat quietly in our stuffy classroom watching his *Death of a Legend*. Teachers are supposed to be above emotions, but my eyes misted when the plane dropped from the sky, bullets flew, and bright wolf blood stained the frozen lake. I never met Bill Mason, but I felt that I knew him.

One day, the letter carrier dropped an envelope at our door. On the back was a logo, the letter "M" sprouting up from the thwarts of a red cedar-strip canoe. The letter inside read:

Feb. 6, 1987

Dear Wendy and Ken:
A mutual friend told me that you are both very familiar with the Tatshenshini River and that you would be able to advise me on its degree of difficulty for an open canoe. I would greatly appreciate it if you would give me some idea. It sounds like an incredible river. Almost too good to be true . . .
Thanks,
Bill Mason

Bill Mason died of cancer before he had the chance to paddle the Tatshenshini and Alsek. Now these rivers, evolving natural masterpieces, are threatened by the march of "progress," the march to exploit our few remaining wild areas. I feel sure that had Bill Mason lived longer, he would have met these mighty rivers and added his clear, strong voice to the chorus speaking out for their preservation.

MAP OF THE RIVERS

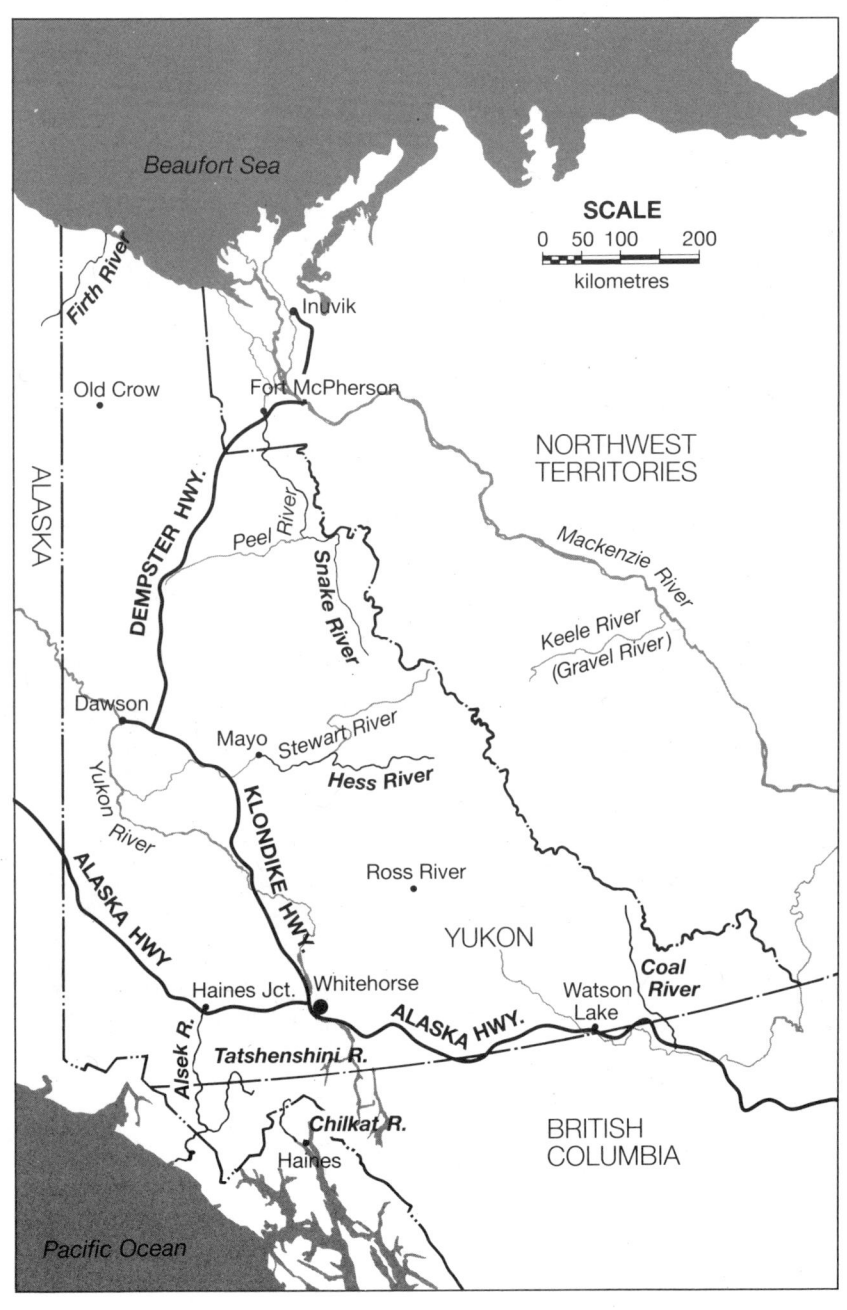

TATSHENSHINI QUEST MAP

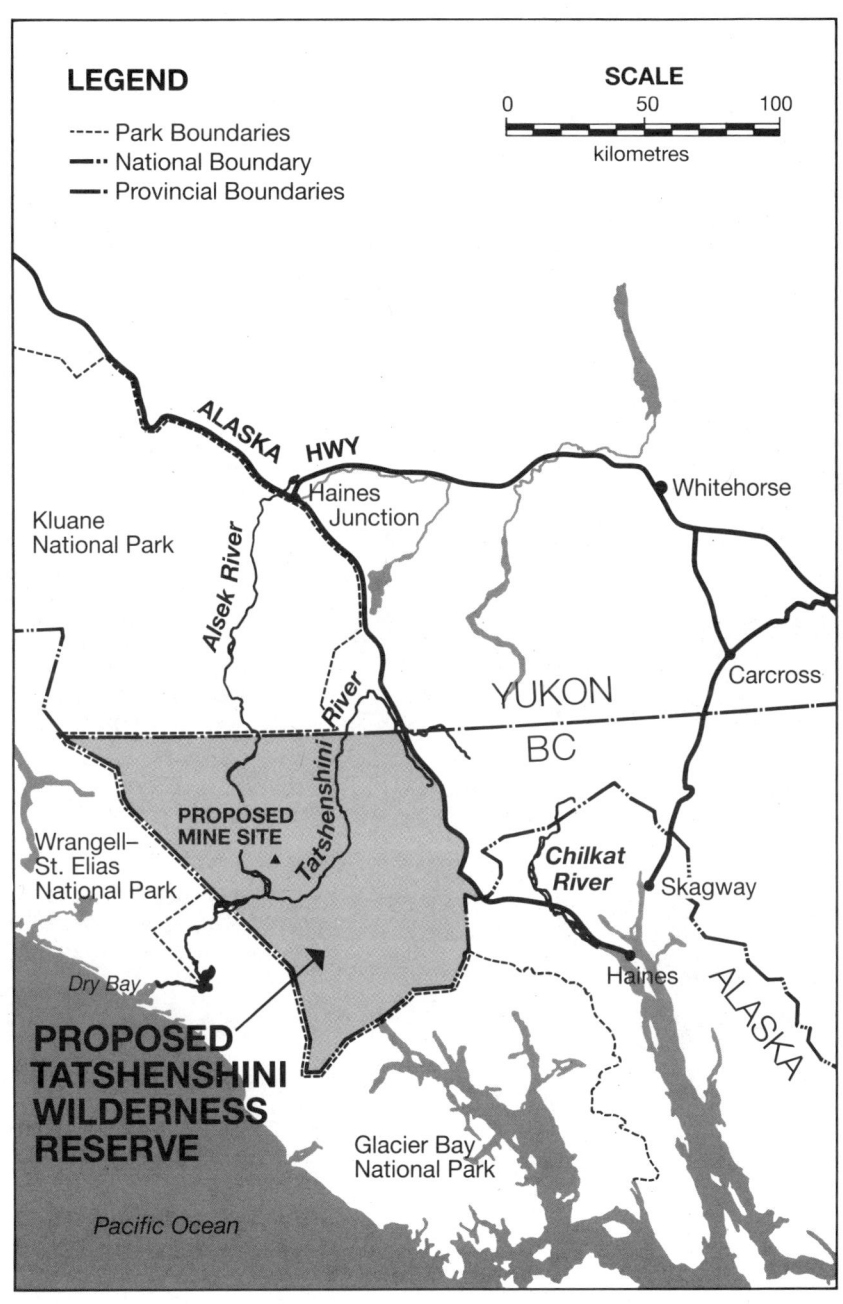

ALSEK RIVER

NO RISK OF BOREDOM

March 1984

My belayer sprawls in the pencil-thin shadow of a Joshua tree on the desert floor. The rope caresses the hot granite and spirals up to the figure-eight knot in my harness. I grab a sloping handhold and jam my foot into the crack, hesitate, and retreat to the ledge. Step up, hesitate, retreat. I try to find a rhythm that I've forgotten over the winter, but I'm clutching the rock, not trusting my feet. A lizard scrabbles past me, clinging effortlessly to the sharp crystals. I flex my fingers and wish that it was John's lead.

I look down. Someone stands beside John, two-dimensional from this height, squat and toadlike. The newcomer shades his eyes with his hand and yells, "Try laybacking, it looks easy."

"Sure," I think. "Just layback it. Just put my feet up by my hands and lean out and layback it. Sure."

On the ground, John listens to a monologue. He is fascinated by other people and is good at getting them to talk about themselves . . . but this time he doesn't need to work at it. Gusty winds blow most of the man's words into the cactus and yucca, but snatches float up to my ledge.

". . . the first ascent, and then I . . ."

I squint at the crack and wipe my sweaty hands on my shorts. I wonder how we'll manage to climb El Capitan if I can't even get up this blob of granite.

". . . frozen waterfalls in Alaska that no one else had the nerve . . ."

The crack is too wide to jam my hand in, so I expand my fist and slowly put my weight on it. There is no way I'm going to layback it.

" . . . get back from Pakistan, I'm going to kayak down the Alsek to Turnback Canyon . . ."

It is here in the desert of Southern California, about as far removed from water as you can get, that I first hear of Turnback Canyon.

The next morning we pile our ropes, boots, and climbing hardware into John's van, and drive north past the billboards that hide the Sierras. In the summer the hills will be kiln-dried but now they are misted with new grass and dotted with bright orange poppies.

Yosemite is a rock climber's Mecca, but a storm hangs over the valley. Low clouds hide the summit of Half Dome, and dark streaks of water spill like tears down the face of El Capitan. We have a long wait before we can start up its vertical 1000-meter "Nose."

When we finish climbing, John drives me to the San Francisco airport. He plans to travel slowly up the Oregon coast and north to Calgary. I have to return to the Yukon to work. I jet from blooming azaleas and warmth to patches of dirty snow and a biting wind that whips along the Yukon River.

July 1986

Six a.m. The sound of the telephone is harsh. I bury my face in the blankets, but the ringing is insistent. Numbed by sleep, I stumble to the kitchen and pick up the receiver. "Is this Ken?" says a voice so quiet I can barely hear it. "John has fallen."

"What?"

"This is John's fiancée." There is a long pause, then the words rush out. "John fell from Mt. Temple. You were his closest friend. He would have wanted me to tell you. He's dead."

Our friendship refuses to go away, like the remembered nerves of a recently amputated arm.

It doesn't feel right to plan big climbs with a different partner. I still need the excitement, the edge that bound John and I together, but I no longer feel comfortable on rock. In kayaking I find an alternate outlet for my energy.

Raven at thirty below.

December 1988

Whitehorse was named for breaking waves in the Yukon River that looked like the flowing manes of galloping horses. These "white horses" are now buried under Schwatka Lake, behind a hydro dam. In the winter the water boils out from the turbines, preventing the river from freezing for miles downstream. On cold mornings, steam rises from the water and billows upward.

Nine o'clock in the morning and it's still dark as I walk into town. Icicles freeze the wool scarf to my chin, and my eyelashes together. A raven squats on a lamppost encrusted with hoarfrost, feathers fluffed against minus thirty temperatures. My shoes squeak against the snow. I see pencils of smoke rising from houses and smell the sharp tang of burning wood. The world beyond that unnaturally illuminated by streetlights is inky black.

The radius of my knowledge about the Alsek River is as well defined as the area lit by the streetlights. I've paddled the rivers that form its headwaters many times, the Kathleen and Dezadeash. They are bright in my memory, but the Alsek is dark and mysterious. I pull open the door of the Yukon Archives, find a table, and cover it with my mitts, sweater, toque, and jacket. I thumb through the card catalogue, but there are only three entries for the Alsek.

I open a xeroxed copy of a *Sports Illustrated* article almost twenty years old, "Caught up in a Hell of White Water." The author is Walt Blackadar, M.D. He lived in Idaho, where kayakers cut their teeth on big water. The story is written as a journal. I think it's exaggerated. Hope it's exaggerated.

My birthday — 49! Looked in the mirror and realized I wasn't getting any younger. Decided to paddle the Alsek alone, though it is against sanity and all safety codes. I've tried for six months to get others to join me.

I have left a letter at home with instructions to spend up to $5,000 to prove me alive or dead ... If I am found dead, the pilot has been told to bury me there and not bring me home but to take positive identification to my wife. — Walt Blackadar

Blackadar was the first kayaker to paddle Turnback Canyon. His solo trip in 1971 gave him, and the Alsek, legendary status. In the 1970s and 1980s, only three other groups ran the canyon, though many looked at the rapids and portaged. Several parties retreated upriver when the surging Tweedsmuir Glacier was too broken up to allow portaging. A young French kayaker drowned during an international expedition in 1981.

Summer 1989

I talk with paddlers and Kluane Park wardens who say Turnback Canyon is unrunnable when the river swells with summer melt, who say it's bad at any flow, who say "Why don't you run the Tatshenshini instead?"

I ignore the advice and decide to paddle the Alsek in late September when the cool nights will turn off the taps of glacial melt from the St. Elias Mountains.

In the past few years, Whitehorse has exploded with enthusiasm for kayaking. Usually, too many people want to go on trips, but this isn't a problem now. Some of my friends can't get the time off work, some insist on hanging up their paddles for the season at the end of August, some just stare at me as though I'm nuts. It looks as though, like Blackadar, I'll have to go solo.

I act blasé so my daughters and close friends won't worry about me. During the daytime I convince even myself that the whole thing is no big deal, but at night my fears surface. I dream of whirlpools that suck my kayak backwards, spinning me as violently as sticks I'd thrown into rain-swollen gutters as a kid. I awake soaked with sweat and squeezing my pillow for flotation.

Wendy Boothroyd, my partner, questions my motives. I try to sort out why I feel driven to go down the Alsek. John and I had also talked about our motivation for doing "high risk" activities.

I first met John at the British Columbia Outward Bound School in 1979. Mouthing platitudes was part of the role that most instructors played. "You can't let fear run your lives," we would earnestly tell our students. "In order to live free, you must be able to accept risk." John was too honest to wholeheartedly join the game. He would listen with a wry smile and ask embarrassingly direct questions. After a couple of months, the School Director told him he didn't have what it takes to be a full instructor.

John left to finish his law degree and we met during breaks to climb. All knees and elbows, he was gangly on the ground, but graceful on rock. We complemented each other; I was stronger on strenuous pitches, he had more nerve on a hard-to-protect pitch. After several seasons of training, we decided to try a big, multi-day rock climb.

We sat on a ledge, three-quarters of the way up El Capitan, tied into the granite with a web of ropes. John was always skinny, but after three days on the face, he looked gaunt. His legs were like vermicelli noodles sticking out of his shorts.

"There's some risk in everything that's important," I said.

"Do you want any more smoked oysters?" he asked. I shook my head. He dripped the oil from the can on a stoned wheat thin, and licked the last drops. He was incapable of putting on fat, no matter what he ate. "You aren't going to pretend that scrabbling up a rock face is important," he said.

"Maybe it isn't," I answered, "But who's to say what has value?" I checked our anchors again.

John Hammond halfway up El Capitan.

We sat in comfortable silence, watching the play of light against the Cathedral Rocks. The valley floor changed from meadow green to a dark olive, and faded from sight as the light escaped to the sky. Stars gleamed, brightly reassuring. My biggest fear was not the climbing itself, but that a storm would pin us down before we reached the top.

"It's funny," I said. "Others fall or get munched by rockfall, but I can't imagine it happening to me."

"Not me," he said. "I don't think I'll live past forty."

"At least you won't die of boredom." We laughed.

At the end of August, I finally find someone interested in the Alsek. I've met Derek Endress a couple of times, at the local rock climbing crags and at the play waves on the Yukon River. He has just finished a summer of smoke-jumping and he's enthusiastic at the thought of a wilderness trip. "You're on your own in Turnback Canyon though," he says.

September 1989

We drive west on the Alaska Highway. It's the first day of autumn, but in the north the change of seasons comes earlier. On the mountains, the edge of new snow is just above us. A few stubborn leaves still dangle from alders bordering the river.

We unload in a gravel pit next to the river. A maple leaf flag flutters above a metal plaque commemorating the Alsek as a "Canadian Heritage River." I would be more impressed if I didn't know that only the section of the river already protected in Kluane National Park has been given this status, if I didn't know that British Columbia did not even make a pretence of joining this federal river protection program.

As we begin our trip it's sunny and cool and the river looks low, but cirrus clouds signal a change. Thick clouds build. Soon we are paddling in a driving rain while gusty winds blow sand and grit across the river. High on scree slopes, Dall sheep and mountain goats seem impervious to the storm. Mountains, shrouded with shifting mist and curtains of rain, keep a tenuous hold on hanging glaciers. Waterfalls spout from gloomy cliffs.

On our first night out we stop on a beach sheltered by alder thickets and orange-hued lava outcrops. Derek wanders into the bush for a final pee before going to bed. "Fuck," he says, walking quickly towards me and looking over his shoulder. "A grizzly, right by our kayaks!" We dive for the tent, feeling vulnerable behind the thin nylon.

The S-bends in Turnback Canyon.

Derek Endress portages through the mists of the Tweedsmuir Glacier.

I look at the bear's tracks in the morning. Derek and the grizzly had both made an about-face when they saw each other. Derek and I had retreated into the dubious security of the tent, the bear to the security of the bush. My foot slides into the print of its hind paw, with room to spare.

It's still raining on the third evening as we arrive at Turnback Canyon, sandwiched between Mt. Blackadar and the Tweedsmuir Glacier. The edge of the glacier is a moonscape of jumbled boulders and gluey muck. We pitch our tent on the exposed moraine. Boisterous squalls shake the tent and fling my paddle into a newly formed pond behind our camp. The downpour loosens refrigerator-sized boulders and chunks of ice from an icefall across the Alsek. They somersault into the river with thunderous roars.

I huddle in my sleeping bag. I've never felt so insignificant.

In the morning the storm is gone, leaving behind a pale sky and a river that is a flooding sea of chocolate milk. The rapids look awful. I'm disappointed, but relieved. I have an excuse not to paddle into the canyon by myself. I can say that the river was just too high, not that I was just too frightened.

Our portage is a two-day slog across the ice and through the labyrinth of shifting boulders that forms the glacier's terminal moraine. We put our kayaks back in the river and the rain chases us the rest of the way down the Alsek, past the icebergs in Alsek Lake, and to the gravel airstrip at Dry Bay.

Winter-Spring 1990

I follow a path of trodden snow beside the Yukon River. The only open water for kilometers glistens in the reflected lights of the Whitehorse Dam. "Turnback Canyon didn't look that bad," I think. "Maybe this spring . . . if high water doesn't hit too early and if the river isn't plugged with avalanche debris . . ."

Leaving my friends to their cross-country skis, I drive Wendy's aging truck, the Sagwagon, to Skagway to board a south-bound Alaska ferry.

Northern California in April. I smear sun screen on my face to protect my tuna-fish northern complexion. Hummingbirds hover over blossoming madrone trees and cold water falls through steep boulder gardens. The Californicated network of highways gives access to whitewater rivers in all shapes and sizes.

Derek also wants to warm up for Turnback Canyon. He busses down to meet me and we kayak nine to five. No weekends off.

A paddling friend, Ian Pineau, flies to Vancouver, rents a car, and drives non-stop down Interstate-5. Ian is known as a cool kayaker, a late graduate of the crash and burn school of paddling. I remember watching from shore as he drifted broadside towards a turbulent slot between two huge boulders. He glanced up and cooly said, "This is not the way to run this rapid."

Ian is in midseason form. I wait in an eddy below the second "falls" in Burnt Ranch Gorge. Locals still talk about the paddler who inadvertently ran the right side of this rapid several years ago. "It wasn't a pretty sight," they say. Now Ian drops through that same chute and becomes a local legend. A foaming cross wave smashes his kayak into a wall and grinds it down the rock face. Ian rolls up in the pool below the rapid with a casual smile. Later he says, "I'd like to join you on the Alsek."

After several weeks California feels like a gigantic water slide park. I think more and more often about another river: one without a paralleling road, without derelict bridges, without beer cans floating in the eddies.

Ian jets home. Derek and I motor through Oregon, Washington, and British Columbia. We arrive in Whitehorse, tired and dusty. A few minutes later, I'm in the kitchen hugging Wendy. When we catch our breath, she says, "You're supposed to call Rod Leighton. I think he wants to paddle Turnback Canyon with you."

Rod is the last word in exercise fanatics, never fully relaxed unless all stores of muscular ATP are depleted. Rod is a solid kayaker, but he hasn't paddled since the summer. "Forget finesse," he says as we discuss Turnback Canyon, "I've been working out, I'll just paddle full speed ahead."

Our camp is a desert island in an ocean of snow and ice.

May 1990

Derek's legs wave from his kayak like the probing tentacles of a squid. I walk gingerly through the jumble of spray decks, bags of food, and assorted gear that make the gravel bar look like a refugee camp. "Hey Derek," I say. "You're supposed to get in the cockpit feet first."

Rod stares at the mountain of gear that he still has to pack. "I'll never fit all this stuff in my kayak," he says mournfully.

The water temperature is barely above freezing, and I'm grateful for the sunshine. But the weather doesn't seem real. The sky is blue but brittle-looking, as though it will shatter and rain as it had when I was on the river last September. The skies stay clear though, and in the four days it takes to reach the canyon the river rises steadily with snow melt. I'm worried that it's already too high but I don't want to say anything.

Winter flexes its muscle as we near the Tweedsmuir Glacier. There is no sign of the moraine, just snowy humps that flatten into a sixteen-kilometer-wide ramp flowing from the mountains. Only in the still air does the intense sunshine give the illusion of warmth. We find a wedge of sand and gravel just wide enough for our tents, a desert island in an ocean of snow and ice.

We're anxious to scout the rapids. The snow covering the moraine is soft and sticky. The crust supports us for a couple of steps, then collapses and we sink to our hips. We look at the first rapids, the S-bends, from the canyon walls. The river is a long way down and it's impossible to get a feel for its size. This was where the young French kayaker had begun his deadly swim. "It doesn't look too bad," says Ian.

We lurch to the next promontory. "That must be Dyna-flow," says Derek, reaching into his pack for the binoculars.

Suddenly, I was in a frothy mess that was far worse than anything I have ever seen... Very narrow — like trying to run down a coiled rattler's back, the rattler striking at me from all sides. I was shoved to the left bank about an inch from the cliff where a foot-wide eddy existed. For perhaps a mile I skidded and swirled and turned down this narrow line. I kept telling myself, "You can roll in this," but all the time I knew I couldn't. — Walt Blackadar

"Jesus," says Derek, passing the binoculars to me. Dyna-flow leaps out at me through the lens. Enormous waves pillow from the walls in slow motion. I can't see any way to get through it upright, and I don't think I could roll in the unpredictably surging boils. I hand the binoculars to Ian and sit down on a boulder sticking out of the snow. Rod clambers across the moraine and kicks steps in a steep snow slope leading to water level.

Derek and Ian talk as though they're giving up on the canyon, mentally adjusting to the long portage across the glacier. I feel the same, but I don't say anything. It seems, somehow, that my dream to paddle the canyon will survive as long I don't express my doubts out loud.

Years earlier, I'd told John that I couldn't imagine an early death. Now I think about it. I wonder if he had looked up from his last belay station and worried about the mountain as I now worry about the river. Or if he assumed, as he had many times before, that this wasn't the time he'd die. He probably didn't think about it. He probably just wanted to climb quickly to the summit, to get out of the cold wind, to drive home.

Ian hands back the binoculars and I focus in. Rod is now standing near the river giving a sense of scale to the whitewater. What had looked like three-meter waves shrink to half that size. The boils are wicked, but not impossible.

Rod climbs back up the slope. "It's just class IV," he reports intently. "Really, if Dyna-flow was on another river, you wouldn't even think about not running it."

I forget my morbid thoughts. Derek and Ian cheer up. We agree to run the S-bends, and at least as far as Dyna-flow. If the Alsek is too much for us, it will be possible to haul our kayaks out of the canyon where Rod climbed down.

Derek packs the binoculars away. The rest of the trip, whenever anyone wants to describe something ugly, binocular is *the* adjective. "Yeah, that's a binocular-sized hole." It's sure to raise a laugh, like an adolescent in-joke that our parents don't understand.

May 10, 1990

Ian rolls over in his sleeping bag. Struggling for more sleep is futile so I unzip the fly and look out. The Tweedsmuir Glacier looms above the other tent. The river seems peaceful.

We've decided that fully loaded boats would be too sluggish in the canyon. We pack tents, sleeping bags, and enough food for the day. The bulk of our stuff is heaped on the gravel spit. Tomorrow we'll hike back across the glacier to retrieve our baggage, dragging a kayak as a cargo sled.

Our movements are slow and deliberate; no one is in a hurry to start paddling. Rod sits on his kayak and, with surgical precision, slices duct tape to protect the raw spots on his hands. Ian sits by the stove, brewing another pot of thick coffee. Derek and I wander back and forth between the pile of gear and our kayaks, making minor adjustments that don't matter. Our conversation is mundane. We don't talk about the canyon. Finally, there is nothing more we can do and we squeeze into our boats.

Caffeine and adrenaline make a potent mixture. We pinball down the Alsek, bouncing from eddy to eddy and loosening our muscles — but our nerves are taut. The rock walls grow, blocking the sunlight. We gather in an eddy. The Alsek is big; the first rapid in the S-bends is big; the canyon walls are big. I feel small. This doesn't seem like the same river that we looked at from above.

I plant my blade in the current, feeling the strength of the river through the paddle shaft. Zooming towards a huge surging hole, I cut right on a tongue that surfs me through the boils.

Until now, I'd been philosophical about safety. We're experienced adults, aware of the dangers. Now I begin to worry. Derek, Rod, and Ian had been swept along in the wake of my enthusiasm. They would be at home, buffered from the elements, but for my obsession with the Alsek. Rod joins me in the eddy, then Derek.

"Good paddling," I say, but Derek is looking upriver.

"Ian's over!" he yells.

After scouting, I ran the first mile of rapids with tremendous respect — found myself upside down twice . . . Slammed into the cliff once and was pinned there for a lifetime . . . flipped and hung upside down while the boat was tossed out of the most violent boils before rolling up . . . — Walt Blackadar

Ian's kayak bounces over a wave. He rolls up. Flips. Rolls up. And flips again as the surging current flattens his boat against a rock wall. We watch silently from the eddy, impotent to help. The boat, held firmly by the river, twitches erratically as Ian tries to right himself. Finally he wallows up, escapes the boils, and joins us. He looks serene, as if he's been splashing in a warm bathtub.

We pull our boats onto a shelf of snow to scout Dyna-flow. The rapid is intimidating. Rod's footprints from yesterday meander up the snow slope. It's the last chance to bail out of the canyon, but everyone wants to stay on the river. No one flips in Dyna-flow.

The rapids are manageable, but I can't shake the awe of being in the canyon. The vertical rock walls pinch in. We find an eddy, but there is no place to wriggle out of our kayaks. I stretch my neck for a look downstream. Towering waves, but no major rapids.

The strong upstream current in the eddy floats me to the others, clustered under a rocky ledge. "I can't see anything horrible for the next hundred meters," I say. "I'm comfortable paddling until we find another eddy. What do you think?"

"I'm comfortable with that," Ian replies, no tremor in his voice. Rod and Derek echo that they're comfortable. We're all comfortable. The Keystone Cops go paddling.

There's one huge horrendous mile of hair (the worst foamy rapids a kayaker can imagine), 30 feet wide, 50,000 cubic feet per second and a 20-degree downgrade going like hell. Incredible! I didn't flip in that mile or I wouldn't be writing.
— Walt Blackadar

An eddy is a safe, social place. A secure place, a place to temporarily shake off the isolation of being alone in a kayak. I leave the eddy, and for the moment, I'm only concerned about myself.

I look for a place to stop, but there isn't one. The Alsek accelerates. The waves are growing, but they're easy to ride. I sink into a trough and look up at the next wave. It doesn't look good — it's too rounded, too regular — but there is nowhere else to go. I reach the top and stare down, a long way down, into a wall of white that spans the river. "Oh shit," I think.

I wish, with Ian-like presence of mind, I'd calmly told myself, "Darn, this is not the way to run this rapid."

With instinctive hope, I drop into the abyss and reach downstream with my paddle. Next thing I know, I'm riding the hole sideways, its crest foaming over my head.

The others leave the eddy at precise intervals. Rod washes over the wave and gazes down at the top of my helmet. He powers into the right side of the maw, avoiding jackhammering me into the depths. Ian gets a great vista — the underside of Rod's boat, and me, still hanging on.

A right-to-left kick of the current bounces me into boily upwellings against the wall. I've never been in a hole that big, and I'm shaky. Rod's kayak flushes out, but Ian is spending quality time in the hole. The end of his kayak spins like a carrot in a blender, until eventually his boat submarines downstream. Derek is the last to drop into the hole. He joins the upside-down parade. I follow.

The rapid Blackadar named Hair.

The cross waves and boils seem friendly compared to what's ahead, tonnes of water nozzling through a five-meter slot. Ghastly froth hugs the wall on the right. Balancing on a tiny tongue that leads past the hole, I claw to escape, but get sucked back, slam into the wall, cartwheel, and roll up. Once. Twice.

I wash out and roll up, relieved to be in my boat, in control, in calmer water. But just downstream, Derek is swimming, clutching Rod's grab loop. His kayak vanishes around the corner. Ian's spray deck is off and he's up to his armpits in water. As he struggles to maneuver his reluctant, submerged kayak into an eddy, it looks as though his pulse rate has finally gone into three figures.

The sun shines brightly. Silty water ebbs and surges impersonally. Our environment is unchanged, but not our situation. Derek is stuck on the wrong side of Turnback Canyon, without a boat. He sits on a sloping shelf of gray rock, catching his breath. "What do we do now?" he asks despondently.

I hesitate for a moment. We are all healthy — not necessarily happy, but healthy. It's prudent to keep it that way. I look downstream. The river pillows off a headwall and accelerates into another constriction. I'm not willing to chase Derek's boat without scouting.

Ian up-ends his boat and water gushes out. Derek scrambles up a promontory so he can see around the corner. "The rapid is short," he yells. "It empties into a calm bay."

"I'll go after his boat," I say to Ian and Rod, "while you ferry Derek over to the moraine."

The next couple of rapids are easy, short chutes that punctuate the widenings of "The Hourglass." I find big eddies, but no kayak. The rock walls pinch in again and I decide that it's not the place to split the group further. I pull into shore to wait. Meanwhile, Derek leaps into the frigid river and Rod and Ian tow him to the other side.

Bleak glacial moraine extends to the river's edge. Snow lies in sodden heaps over the rock and ice. I walk back to meet Derek while Rod and Ian scout the next rapids. Derek looks out of place trudging across the waste in his dripping spray skirt, clutching a paddle.

In his place I would be tired and discouraged, and he looks it. I try to feel empathetic, but I can't force it. Too much of me is wondering about the rest of the canyon.

"We should camp as soon as we find a decent spot," I say, looking around.

"What about the boat?" His voice is tight.

I try to think of something reassuring to say, but all I can remember are the words of a veteran paddler, old enough and experienced enough to be able to rise above the embarrassment of swimming, but perceptive enough to understand how it feels. "There are two types of boaters," he'd said in a grizzled voice, "those who have swum, and those who will swim — and they're the same thing." I know something like that would sound banal. I keep quiet.

We arrange to meet above the Last Major Constriction, the final big rapid in the canyon. Ian, Rod, and I set off. We're increasingly conservative. I feel drained of adrenaline, of energy. Even the caffeine has worn off.

Steep moraine and tangled alder kill any thought of camping at The Constriction. On the top of a ridge, Derek is a tiny silhouette. We gesture to him with our paddles, waving them and pointing downstream. He doesn't move but leans on his paddle, radiating dejection. I feel guilty as we ride easily on the current, wondering whether we could have found a campsite with a thorough search.

The last rapids are straightforward. Fortunately. Our adventure quotas are filled for the day.

This has been a day! I want any kayaker to read my words well! The Alsek gorge is unpaddleable! Unbelievable . . . I'm not coming back. Not for $50,000, not for all the tea in China. Read my words well and don't be a fool. It's unpaddleable. — Walt Blackadar

Alsek whitewater.

Rest stop on the Tweedsmuir Glacier.

Ian looks at Rod and me. "Congratulations," he says. I smile, but without the euphoria I had expected. We are the first all-Canadian group to paddle the "unpaddleable" Turnback Canyon, but we're four boaters with three boats — in the middle of an icy wilderness. I worm through the underbrush and onto the moraine. Rod and Ian stay behind to organize gear. I whoop and hear an answering shout. A tiny splash of color moves slowly towards me over the monochrome landscape.

Derek slumps on a boulder and stares at his feet. "Now what?"

"It's not an emergency." I say. "We have plenty of food and gear at our cache." I'm trying to imagine how I would have reacted to a potentially lethal swim, to the cold, to the exertion, to the sight of us successfully paddling the canyon while he walked along the bank. He hasn't tried to hide his feelings, but at the same time he has maintained his composure.

"What about my kayak?"

"Someone will have to stay here while the others paddle out to radio for a helicopter. Hopefully we'll find the boat along the way."

Derek's face sags at the thought of waiting by himself.

"Look," I say, "I don't mind staying here. You can paddle my kayak."

"Let me think about it." His expression says that it's settled.

We search the alder-infested bedrock shelves overlooking the glacier, and find two snow-free tent sites. The clear sky brings a dry night but plummeting temperatures. Derek's sleeping bag is in his kayak. He borrows a sleeping pad and swaths himself, mummy-like, in spare clothing.

May 11, 1990

A ptarmigan flutters over the tent, its guttural croak echoing Ian's snores. I hear the quavering whistle of a varied thrush and the harsh scream of a hawk. The border of alder buffering the river from the glacier stirs with life — a contrast to our last camp. There, only wind, rock fall, and river rumblings punctuated the silence.

We zigzag over the moraine, heading back to our base camp at the head of the canyon. Derek, whose boots are adrift, ranges ahead in wet-suit booties, scouting for the best route. Rod and Ian shackle themselves to my kayak, like prisoners in a chain gang, and drag it. Fearing snow blindness, we fashion glacier goggles from duct tape. We walk gingerly on the untrustworthy crust of snow, crawling up steep slopes: hands, knees, and feet grappling for support. The going is easier when we reach the glacier itself.

Our camp is now an island. The rising river has marooned us on the verge of the glacier.

"No problem," says Rod. "All we do is ferry back and forth."

He strides to the water. Derek wriggles into the kayak. Ian and I squat in the snow, content to watch. Rod sits on the stern deck, legs hooked around Derek's waist. Ian and I begin to giggle. As they wallow into the water, the stern deck collapses. Rod sinks into the numbing water. "Paddle faster!" he screeches. The water reaches crotch level. "Brace, brace! Paddle harder!"

"I am paddling hard." Derek sounds indignant.

"Paddle harder!"

Paddle harder!

Ian and I walk upstream, still laughing, and ford knee-depth shallows to the island.

Derek burrows into Rod's sleeping bag to catch up on sleep. I light the stove and brew coffee. Rod lolls back on his sleeping pad. "Where does Detour Creek flow into the Tatshenshini?" he asks. None of our maps extend to the Tatshenshini.

"Somewhere above Windy Craggy," I answer, feeling lazy.

We sip our coffee. The sun heats our strip of exposed gravel and heat waves distort the mountains at the head of the glacier. Ian takes off his shirt. "How far it is up the Tatshenshini to Dalton Post?" Rod asks.

Rod Leighton begins his walk home.

Neither Ian nor I know.

"I wonder how long it would take someone to walk to the highway from here?" Rod has a faraway expression in his eyes.

"A hell of a long time," I reply.

"And it would take someone awfully stupid," Ian says.

We laugh, but I look at Rod and realize where this is leading. He is determined to walk upriver, climb over the mountains to the Tatshenshini, and eventually back to the Haines Road.

We gather late in the afternoon, at the head of our island. Rod puts on his dry suit and plunges into the water. Ian ferries him across the Alsek and he walks out of sight to the north.

Five days later, he hobbles into Dalton Post. Five days of sinking to his armpits in soft snow. Five days of crawling through willows and alders, and scrambling up rotten rock pitches. Five days of watching the slopes for spring avalanches and the thickets for grizzlies.

Derek, Ian, and I lurch across the moraine one last time. We somehow squeeze our gear, and Rod's extras, into our boats. I duct tape the extra paddle to my stern deck, like a mutant rudder left behind by the march of kayak evolution.

I don't expect to find Derek's kayak before the river widens at Alsek Lake, but a few kilometers below the canyon we see a familiar yellow shape. It bobs under an ice floe, brimming with sand and slightly abraded. Derek caresses his boat. Love holds no grudges. We take turns towing the spare kayak.

The Alsek wilderness casts a powerful spell and soon Turnback Canyon is a memory, an image of dark rock walls and surging whitewater. Winter turns into spring as we escape the refrigerator chill of the Tweedsmuir Glacier. Snow retreats to higher slopes. The greens of new leaves lie in a delicate spray over the trees.

I think about John and wonder why it isn't enough to just travel in this wilderness. We could have floated the Tatshenshini to reach this glaciated land of rugged peaks. I enjoy leisurely trips, once in a while . . . but then, the country seems to flow past like a movie. Why do I need a physical challenge to make the colors vivid, the scenes real?

But I do, and already I'm thinking about a new adventure.

Small people, large moraine.

Postscript - August 1990

In midsummer I again float on the icy waters of the Alsek.

Five of us have just finished the "first descent" of the Bates River, although lengthy portages around difficult rapids made our river trip more of a backpacking jaunt encumbered with kayaks. The Bates flings us into the Alsek just above Turnback Canyon.

We're drenched by a frigid drizzle as we put up our tents on the verge of the Tweedsmuir Glacier. The toe of the glacier looks like a gigantic whale's back rising from the river and disappearing into the mist. Our world is a cold gray sphere: the summit of Mt. Blackadar is obscured and Turnback Canyon is hidden by a curtain of rain.

It's midsummer in the north and the glaciers of the largest non-polar icefields in the world are sweating water thick with silt and as cold as January. The Alsek is booming and we have no intention of running the canyon.

The next morning the fog dissipates, the sun comes out, and we carry our kayaks into the chaos of shifting boulders and slimy mud that makes up the terminal moraine of the Tweedsmuir Glacier. The horizon of ice looks motionless as it flows towards us and the St. Elias Mountains shimmer in a blue haze. To the west, the Alsek is invisible, but I feel its presence as it slams through the canyon.

Working in pairs, we hoist a heavily loaded kayak and clip it into padded slings around our shoulders. We trudge over the loose rocks, drop the boat, and return for the next load. The intense sun turns the moraine into a giant reflector oven. There isn't a scrap of shade for kilometers. Two strenuous days later, dehydrated and hungry, we finally reach a steep slope leading back to the river.

"We've already carried these boats for seventeen and a half hours," says Poco glumly, looking at the rock and ice between us and the water. Poco is from California, a land where portages are short and the nearest highway is usually only a stone's throw away.

We sit down to rest and pass around slices of logan bread spread thickly with cream cheese. I lay back, lean my head against my kayak, and close my eyes. This land has a timeless quality that leaves me feeling fragile. It's as though we've paddled backwards through a time warp and landed in the last ice age.

A mechanized whirring clashes with the harmonious sounds of wind in the rocks and the deep pulsing of the river. I look up. A helicopter hovers over the shoulder of Mt. Blackadar, banks over the river, and returns to its lair at Geddes Resources' exploration camp at Windy Craggy Mountain. Although the access road to this proposed mega-project would follow the Tatshenshini, the ore body itself is just on the other side of the mountains flanking Turnback Canyon.

If the probing fingers of development are touching even this remote and rugged wilderness, what land is safe?

TATSHENSHINI RIVER

TATSHENSHINI WILDERNESS QUEST

Two views of the world . . .

One of the world's greatest river systems — that of the Alsek and its main tributary, the Tatshenshini — is all but unknown in its own homeland. The two rivers forge their channels by slicing through the massive coastal mountains of the inside arc of the Gulf of Alaska. The St. Elias and Fairweather ranges build to summits between 16,000 and 19,950 feet, including Mount Logan, Canada's highest . . .
— from *Rivergods* (Bangs and Kallen, 1985)

The impact on the wilderness recreation area is a somewhat subjective effect. The area to be traversed by the road is not one of great scenic beauty or abundant recreational use.
— from a presentation by Gerald Harper, President of Geddes Resources, in Whitehorse, Oct. 12, 1989

If you look at topographic maps of the St. Elias Mountain region, you'll see mainly white, the white of permanent snowfields, the white of glaciers. These maps show only isolated belts of forest green that cling to the blue lines of the Tatshenshini River (pronounced TAT-SHEN-SHEE-NEE, but known as the "Tat") and its tributaries.

The forest along the Tat provides a unique corridor of wildlife habitat in a harsh, frozen environment. This is the only Canadian home of the rare glacier bear, a silver-blue subspecies of black bear. Runs of spawning salmon help support one of the world's highest-density grizzly populations. Dall sheep and mountain goats graze on alpine slopes above the river, bald eagles and gyrfalcons soar overhead, and wolves slip quietly through the boreal forest.

As I study the maps, a radio voice in the background is saying that another low-pressure area is brewing in the Gulf of Alaska. Rain will drench the lower flanks of the St. Elias Mountains, and snow will cover the high country like a down quilt, a soft, icy quilt that will compact and flow in huge frozen rivers towards the Tat and Alsek valleys. To ride the meltwater in these valleys is to glimpse a glaciated world that is like an echo of the last ice age.

The Tatshenshini-Alsek wilderness is ringed by national parks — Kluane to the north, Wrangell-St. Elias to the east, Glacier Bay to the south — but the British Columbia section is unprotected. People call it a wilderness by default. It is as though, because bureaucrats haven't pencilled in the dotted lines of park boundaries on maps, its wild nature is undeserved.

A few decades ago, the Tatshenshini was almost unknown. It lived in the memories of Indian peoples, whose ancestors used it as a trading corridor between Dry Bay and the interior, and in the minds of a handful of river runners and prospectors.

In 1958, geologists working for Falconbridge found copper-mineralized boulders and traced them to their source near Windy Craggy Mountain. The deposits seemed rich and claims were staked and registered. But the land was remote, markets were distant, and other sources of copper were plentiful. For several decades the land remained only a gleam in stock promoters' eyes. Eventually, Falconbridge sold the property to Geddes Resources, a Toronto-based company.

In the early 1980s, Geddes Resources conducted further surveys near Windy Craggy. They bulldozed an airstrip out of the alpine tundra and flew in explosives and heavy equipment. Like ambitious, copper-eating moles, they tunnelled several kilometers into the mountain, probing and sniffing the sulphide deposits.

Dall sheep.

As Gerald Harper said in Whitehorse, "The combination of flow through financing and a junior bull market in 1987 provided the opportunity for Geddes to embark on its ambitious program." The fragility of the wilderness was exposed and threatened by a junior bull market, whatever that is.

To reach Windy Craggy, the company proposes to carve a 110-kilometer road through the wilderness and construct a major bridge across the Tatshenshini. On their drawing board are pipelines, an ore concentrator mill, dams, a tailings impoundment lake, and a small city to house workers.

Geddes intends to blast the top off Windy Craggy Mountain. What is now a lofty summit would become a pit six hundred meters deep and more than a kilometer wide. Some view the removal of a mountain as megalomania, as playing God with land that has been patiently shaped by millions of years of natural forces. If environmentalists are unable to stop the mine, the excavation will form a crevice between high points. "We will be creating two mountains," said Gerald Harper to a *Globe and Mail* reporter.

Unfortunately for Geddes Resources, images of the wild Tatshenshini are indelibly etched in the minds of river travellers, images incompatible with tailings dumps and rumbling ore trucks. Paddlers who have descended the Tat compare their experiences with those in the Grand Canyon of the Colorado River. Both rivers have exciting whitewater. Both rivers have stunning natural surroundings. These rugged landscapes breed fiery-eyed wilderness zealots.

Until 1989, only isolated pockets of opposition fought the Windy Craggy mega-project . . . until the organization Tatshenshini Wild became the environmental central nervous system for dozens of groups including the Sierra Club, the Western Canada Wilderness Committee, and the National Audubon Society. Almost overnight, the Tat became a symbol of North America's vanishing wilderness, and Tatshenshini Wild represented more than two million advocates across the continent.

The violation of the Tatshenshini-Alsek wilderness by the proposed mine road is unacceptable to preservationists, but concerns about water pollution caused Geddes' first regulatory setback. Their "Stage I" mine plan was rejected by government because of unproven technology and inadequate attention to acid rock drainage. The quantity and high sulphur content of the ore at Windy Craggy make acid drainage a time bomb that would threaten the Tatshenshini for centuries.

The proponents of the mine are struggling to convince bureaucrats and politicians that they have their finger on the pulse of the latest technology, "state of the art" wizardry that makes environmental disaster an impossibility. And anyway, in these tough economic times, money is more valuable than wilderness. Isn't it?

Geddes officials no doubt anticipated smooth sailing in the seas of regulatory procedures and environmental assessment, but they were soon navigating through angry waves and feeling seasick.

Two views of the world . . .

The mine and seventy-mile road would be devastating to the best remaining wilderness area in the world. The Sierra Club favors the establishment of a Tatshenshini-Alsek Wilderness Preserve of 2.8 million acres which would accomplish the largest contiguous protected wilderness area in the world.
   — Ed Wayburn, Director, Sierra Club (Head, Alaska Task Force)

I think this environmental movement is being orchestrated by a small group of people and I think it is largely orchestrated by people who are not from the local area.
   — Gerald Harper, *Yukon News*, Feb. 28, 1990

December 1990

It's winter in the Yukon and CBC radio is interviewing a scientist from New York who is researching SAD — seasonal affective disorder. In the north we call it "cabin fever." All you need to do, according to the expert, is walk around wearing a special lamp that beams light on your face, light that deactivates the shadows of SAD. I flick off the radio and walk downtown.

Thinking about Windy Craggy gives me SAD, and "Rudolph the Red-nosed Reindeer" piped into the frozen Yukon dark through tinny department store speakers isn't helping. Environmental groups are often criticized because many members are from urban jungles, but the money driving development is from there too. I wonder how I can fight the Toronto Stock Exchange and whether B.C. Premier Vander Zalm reads my letters. Struggling to preserve the Tat is like paddling upstream against a swiftly flowing river of dollars.

Sometimes I feel like shouting, "Screw it!" I have a list of secret streams buried in the wilderness where I can retreat from D-9s, canyons where even the most zealous developer can't find me. A few years ago, the Tat and Alsek were on that list. But wild places are being hunted down like the California grizzly of the 1800s and I don't have the time to hide forever. So I keep organizing meetings and talking to the media and writing letters and chucking the standard "thank you for your concern" replies in the recycling pile.

I brush the frost from my eyebrows, peel the frozen scarf from my nose, and wander into a lounge that exudes a plastic Christmas cheer. Candy canes festoon the walls, a green and red sign glitters Merry Christmas, and someone has pinned up an inflatable Santa. Derek Endress and Ian Pineau walk in, throw their parkas on the backs of chairs, and beckon to the waitress.

In the eight months since we kayaked Turnback Canyon on the Alsek, we've started talking about the Grand Canyon of the Stikine. We're like peewee hockey players daydreaming about skating on National Hockey League ice. The Stikine is major league paddling, and I feel like a bench warmer even considering it.

We've discussed a paddle-a-thon to raise money and publicize the development threats to both the Stikine and the Tat. We don't have definite plans, just a nebulous desire to put something back into the wilderness that has given so much to each of us.

"I called Ric Careless of Tatshenshini Wild today," I say. "He liked our idea of collecting sponsorships for paddling the Tat and the Stikine."

"All right!" says Derek.

"But . . . he feels that this year is the crucial year for the Tat, and he's reluctant to confuse the public with different threats to different rivers."

"That makes sense," says Ian.

"So, I thought," I continue, "that maybe we should postpone the Stikine and confine our paddling extravaganza to the Tat and the Alsek."

"I was psyched for the Stikine," says Ian, looking as though I had just taken away his candy cane, "but I suppose I can wait for a year."

"I have a score to settle with Turnback Canyon," says Derek with a gleam in his eye. "I'd love to go back to the Alsek. And I know Jody will want to go."

"That goes without saying," says Ian.

We decide that the Chilkat River deserves a place in our paddling agenda. The Chilkat flows into the Lynn Canal near Haines, Alaska, and parallels part of the proposed route of ore trucks from Windy Craggy. This will broaden the scope of our plans, and include all the major rivers to be affected if the mine is built. We schedule the Chilkat for May, the Tat for July, and the Alsek for September.

I call the *Yukon News* and the *Whitehorse Star*. I call Haines and Vancouver and Washington D.C. What began as a beer-assisted, midwinter dream balloons into a continent-wide campaign. The World Wildlife Fund supports us under their "Endangered Spaces Program." They'll collect sponsorships for the 675 river kilometers we'll travel and help publicize our crusade.

Someone calls our plan the Tatshenshini Wilderness Quest, and it sticks. Once the Quest is named it ceases its brief life as a dream and grows into something real. We'll be able to make our point by *doing* something, something more tangible than dispatching letters that join the endless paper migration between my door and politicians' desks.

Two views of the world . . .

After the fate of Glen Canyon in Arizona was sealed — literally — by the Bureau of Reclamation dam and reservoir, it was referred to as "the place no one knew." That conservation defeat is a perpetual reminder that remote and grandly beautiful natural areas can be lost all too easily.

American Rivers [a large U.S. organization dedicated to preserving wild rivers] is working to make sure that the little-known Alsek-Tatshenshini river system, one of the most spectacular watersheds in North America, is not lost to a monumentally destructive, $400 million mining scheme.

— from American Rivers Newsletter, Fall 1990

What we are talking about here is the creation of new wealth . . . a project that will really help Canada's foreign exchange balance. It is a project that will open up an entire mining district to development.

— Gerald Harper, *Alaska Business Monthly*, December 23, 1990

July 5-10, 1991

The back lawn is a chaos of paddling gear. Dry suits and life jackets are draped over kayaks like forgotten streamers after a New Year's party. Sue Johnson is dabbing liquid soap on an ancient raft to find out where it's leaking. Jody Schick sands down a patch and Derek walks out the gate to buy more duct tape and glue. We have a serious case of the pre-trip jitters: hoping we've packed enough food, hoping that the repairs to our old rubber raft will last until the ocean, hoping that our friends will remember to feed McAllister the cat while we're away.

Ian, Derek, Jody, and I have invited a dozen companions for the Tat portion of our Quest. It's an eclectic group — friends who have helped with our environmental work, a renowned landscape artist from Central Canada, an Anglican minister from the small Yukon village of Carcross, a university student from British Columbia. Our collective roots come from across Canada, from the Maritimes to the Pacific. Some of us have lived in the Yukon for decades, a few have never before ventured "north of sixty."

Trip preparation brings with it its own stresses, but at least the flotsam strewn around the backyard is tangible evidence that our trip will soon be a reality. For the past several months I've been spinning in a whirlpool of Tatshenshini Wilderness Quest business: giving interviews for radio and television, mailing off magazine articles, motoring through the Pacific states and British Columbia with a slide tour. It will be a relief to plunge my paddle in the water and forget about advocacy for a couple of weeks.

A mouldering log cabin at Dalton Post.

At Dalton Post the first fireweed of the season blooms outside mouldering log cabins. During the 1890s, infamous Jack Dalton guided "cheechakos" (newcomers to the Yukon) from Haines, Alaska, to the Klondike. His specialty was fleecing his customers; charging exorbitant tolls and lightening their excess weight of gold. The clearings beside the Tatshenshini at Dalton Post served as a stopover along the trail.

Long before Dalton's day, Southern Tutchone and Tlingit Indians lived here, fishing, hunting, and trapping along the banks of the Tat. The Champagne-Aishihik Band is currently negotiating its Yukon land claim. They've also served notice to the Canadian and B.C. governments that their interests extend south of the Yukon border and include the area of the proposed Windy Craggy Mine.

Motorhomes and campers are parked outside the log cabins. Scores of people stand on the shore in rubber boots, clutching fishing rods. Ghetto blasters blare and a man walks past with a fifteen-kilogram chinook. This is the only place in the Yukon where you have a realistic chance of hauling in a salmon. The fish are worn after battling the strong currents of the Tatshenshini; they're red and ready to spawn but still have to sneak past the lures that drift through the water seductively.

Since we're used to paddling in small numbers, we've decided to split into two independent groups, each with one raft and attendant kayaks. Our party of eight has little experience with rafts . . . in fact we've always called them pig boats. Now I climb onto the stern with a long canoe paddle. Ontario artist E. Robert Ross, my daughter Kirsten, and Jody's mother Joanne Schick are wedged among our waterproof river bags. Sue Johnson, a bird biologist turned physiotherapist, shoves us into the current.

Wendy Boothroyd and Kate Williams, a Whitehorse art teacher, are already floating around the corner in their kayaks. Jody clips a carabiner onto the grab loop of my kayak and yells, "Someone take a picture of Ken in the pig boat." Jody is a recent high-school graduate, already an accomplished paddler. He will tow my kayak so I can use it after I help the raft through the hardest whitewater.

We have time to practise maneuvering the raft before we hit the rapids. I know it won't react like a kayak, so I pretend that it is a middle-aged canoe that has run to fat. I suggest a back ferry. We edge across the river reluctantly, is if we are paddling a bloated sausage though oatmeal.

"Good job," I yell with an assurance that sounds phony even to me.

The forest gives way to orange bluffs and rock walls. A merganser swims upstream, three ducklings clinging to her back and four others splashing behind. The last reminder of the civilization we're leaving is the zigzag line of an abandoned mining road on alpine slopes to the north.

The whitewater begins slowly, a few riffles and the occasional rock to avoid. The raft doesn't knife through the waves; it molds itself to the shape of the water. Sitting on the pontoons, we rise and fall like children on a carousel. After grinding over several rocks that would have disemboweled a canoe, we learn to take evasive action well above any obstacle.

Our rafting personalities emerge quickly. I'm acting hearty, like the captain of the love boat, trying to exude confidence. Kirsten reads the water well, but she's quiet, reluctant to be pushy with us old folks. Joanne is enthusiastic but respectful of the water. She abandons her paddle and grabs the centre rope whenever anything big and white approaches. Sue and Robert are opposites. Sue is dynamic; Robert is mellow. Sue concentrates on the water, eyes wrinkled with crow's-feet of determination; Robert stops paddling to watch a bald eagle or clouds curling over a ridge.

"There's a rock ahead," yells Sue. "Should we backpaddle?"

"Look at that mountain," says Robert, binoculars welded to his eyes. "I can't believe I was in Hamilton a couple of days ago."

The kayakers probe the rapids ahead, signalling when it's clear, signalling when to pull over to scout. Jody gestures to the right with his paddle and I see a jagged rock wall at the end of a series of standing waves.

"Spin left," I shout. "Okay, backpaddle!"

Our boat is the "Model T" of rafts. No oar frame for us. No self-bailing or inflatable floor. A couple of waves curl over Joanne and slosh around our feet. We sink a bit further and wallow towards the canyon wall. Our angle is good but we're going nowhere against the stiff current.

"Backpaddle hard!" I yell.

We maintain our angle and hit the pillow wave foaming off the rock. Our bow kisses the wall gently, a first-date kiss, and we lurch into an eddy. As we scout the next rapid we hear the shouts of a commercial raft group. Two oared boats give the wall a wide berth but a paddle raft slams into the wall, spins, and grinds across the face. Our raft would have looked like grated cheese after that maneuver, but their space-age fabric seems as good as new as they blunder into the next series of rocks and waves.

"We did better than they did," says Sue.

"This pontoon is really saggy," says Joanne. "We'll need to pump again."

"We should call this thing the Sag Maggot," says Kirsten.

The name sticks.

Later, at camp, we laugh about the day's antics. Joanne ducking under a breaker. Jody towing my kayak into a micro-eddy after it flipped and filled with water. Wendy and Kate blithely paddling into a hole that even the raft avoided. Me bailing the raft, unaware that water was gushing through a rip under the packs.

The Sag Maggot.

"Who's coming hiking?" asks Wendy after breakfast on the third morning.

"I'm going to work on these paintings," says Robert. He has volunteered to do a painting for a small art auction we plan to hold to raise money for our Tat campaign. He'll also work with the World Wildlife Fund to showcase the beauty of this land through his art.

Joanne volunteers to stay behind and bake a surprise birthday cake for Kirsten who turns nineteen today. The rest of us ferry the Sag Maggot across the river and head towards the alpine. Unlike the Alsek just to the north, the Tatshenshini is bordered by forest and thick undergrowth. The meadows offer succulent forage for wildlife, and soon we're treading on thick patches of grizzly and moose manure.

"Here's a bear's day bed," says Wendy, pointing to an oval patch of flattened foliage.

"More likely a moose," I say, looking at the heaping piles of rounded moose pellets.

"Look at that," yells Jody. Above us a pair of golden eagles are playing. They ride the thermals towards the clouds and chase each other in looping spirals. We watch until they vanish behind a ridge.

Grazing mountain goat.

Wading through grasses and flowers.

An alder jungle swallows us and we struggle upwards until it spits us out into lush fingers of meadow. We wade upwards through chest-deep grass and flowers. I let my eyes blur and the individual blossoms become blobs of color, deep purple circles of larkspur and monkshood, green-blossomed orchids, and fiery patches of columbine.

We follow an animal trail to a rocky gully that falls into a creek valley. Below us a mountain goat grazes. We watch and take pictures until it romps into the gully with a clatter of sliding scree and rolling rocks. During our descent into the valley, we collect fistfuls of the goat hair that clings to bushes and thorny brambles like downy blossoms.

"We could spin this hair and knit it into a toque," says Kate.

"We'll be able to sell it at our art auction," suggests Wendy, "a hat with genuine Tatshenshini goat hair."

It's dusky and we're tired as we pile into the raft and paddle back to camp. Black Forest birthday cake revives us. Kirsten opens her birthday present, a purple T-shirt that we bought at a paddling film festival sponsored by the Friends of Bill Mason. There's a wolf on the front and the words *The Cry of the Wild.* "I've never seen a wolf," says Kirsten. "I'd love to see one . . . more than any other animal."

On the way to the tent I find tracks, fresh tracks. "Come here Kirst!" I yell.

She kneels and spreads her hands over the imprints in the wet sand and asks, "What kind of tracks are these?"

"Wolves," I answer, and we follow the tracks until they disappear into the forest.

Two views of the world . . .

Its scenery, wildlife, and wilderness easily make it one of the grandest and most unique places of North America . . .
— Brock Evans, Vice President, National Audubon Society

But you have to look at it in terms of the many beautiful sites in Canada. Is this one of the extremely beautiful ones and is this the last of the wilderness rivers? There's certainly no shortage of rivers. I can name a half dozen rivers that flow into the Arctic that are far more wilderness than the Tatshenshini will ever be.
— Gerald Harper, *Yukon News*, Feb. 28, 1990

July 11, 1991

"Where do they want to build the bridge?" asks Robert.

"Just upstream of the confluence," I answer.

We're camped just below the wide gravel fan of the O'Connor River, the valley the proposed Geddes road would descend. It would then bridge the Tatshenshini and parallel the river for twenty kilometers before winding up Tats Creek to Windy Craggy Mountain. I try to imagine huge ore trucks, one every ten minutes, crossing the river in front of me. I try, but it's impossible.

Near these canyon walls, Geddes Resources would build a bridge.

The rounded red flanks of Carmine Mountain to the west are encircled by a scarflike band of mist. Across the river, serrated ridges point towards the more rugged landscape in the heart of the St. Elias Mountains. Robert is sitting on the bank, painting the panorama to the west: the river, a cliff wall, glaciers looking like blue clouds spilling over the high country. He trades his brush for binoculars and scans the alpine. Already today we've seen five mountain goats, a swan standing on one leg like an albino flamingo, three moose, a lynx calmly sitting on the bank, and dozens of bald eagles.

"Look to the left of those three blobs of snow," says Robert, handing me his binoculars.

A brown dot on the green slope sprouts legs as I focus. A grizzly. North America's largest land predator, a creature superbly adapted to the mountains, a creature geared for survival — at least before humans developed the technological power to destroy mountains, the power to create lakes of acid, the power to destroy species.

The grizzly is too far away to be seen clearly, but it's exhilarating just knowing it's there. It reaffirms that the Tatshenshini is truly wild. A wilderness isn't a wilderness without its large predators.

The Sierra Nevada in California is called a "gentle wilderness," perhaps because the last grizzly was exterminated there in 1922. If that's what it takes for a land to be gentle, then give me the raw, the uncontrolled, the *uncontrollable* every time.

During frontier days in North America, grizzlies, wolves, and even eagles were regarded as dangerous, as evil, as vermin. They were systematically shot, poisoned, trapped, and chased away by habitat loss. Grizzlies have one of the lowest reproductive rates of any North American mammal, making them particularly vulnerable. There haven't been any specific studies of Tatshenshini bears, but in Kluane National Park, female grizzlies don't reach sexual maturity until they are seven years old and have litters only once every three or four years.

The proposed road into Windy Craggy would bisect a huge territory with one of the highest grizzly populations anywhere. The B.C. Ministry of Parks calls the Tat the "only significant unroaded recreational river in B.C." and has expressed concern over the network of cat tracks and exploration roads that predictably hemorrhage when a major access road is cut through a wilderness. More vehicle traffic. More hunting. More poaching.

Poaching of African animals has led species to the brink of extinction. In North America, bears are at risk. Grizzly and black bear gall bladders are dried and crushed to a powder, and sold as medicines in the Far East, as well as in Chinese pharmacies in Canadian cities. Bear paws are boiled, spiced, and ladled into soup bowls. Claws are hot jewelry items. In the Yukon, a man was recently arrested with fifty-eight bear gall bladders. Fifty-eight dead bears.

On the banks of the Tat, we watch the grizzly until lowering clouds draw a gray curtain over the alpine. The next morning we can't see it, but it is there somewhere, a part of the wilderness it depends upon for survival.

Two views of the world . . .

It does not appear that the environmental and engineering problems associated with this project can be resolved with existing technology . . . We believe the long-term environmental degradation likely to result from the proposed Windy Craggy Mine outweighs any economic gains that may accrue.
— Steven Pennoyer, Director, Alaska Region, National Marine Fisheries Service, U.S. Department of Commerce

The rafting industry, they've developed a lot of hype about the wilderness there. There's a lot of B.S. We recognize that people are going to be concerned. We're doing everything we can. But we're not going to be able to satisfy everybody.
— Gerald Harper, *Anchorage Daily News*, December 23, 1990

July 12-13, 1991

The closer we get to the ocean, the wilder the land becomes. The rock walls look unclimbable; the forest looks impenetrable. Steely blue glaciers patiently grind down the mountains and send silt to the ocean via the waterways. Churning muddy water bubbles, hisses, and pops against the side of our boats. The Tat is big, fast, gray, and cold, and it's the only corridor where travel through this land is practical.

As we pull out on a sand bar to scout another rapid, there's a splash and a glimpse of silver. "Did you see that?" asks Robert. "It looked like a shark!"

Salmon are a critical component of the food web of this wilderness. At the beginning of the trip, Kirsten started counting the bald eagles she saw, but lost track after a couple of days: eagles perched on fish carcasses, eagles wheeling above the river, eagles diving into eddies with outstretched talons. Salmon are also an important food source for bears, otters, mink, and for sea lions, orcas, and other marine mammals and birds at the coast.

We want to hike into the alpine to look at the proposed mine site at Windy Craggy Mountain, so we set up camp at the mouth of Tats Creek. Clouds have been playing on the mountains all day, swarming on the summits like children on a jungle gym. Now they melt away. Shafts of sunshine light the rugged slopes. A waterfall is a white gash against the green bush. Downstream, a young black bear forages above a rock wall.

The next morning we walk up the gravel fan that flanks Tats Creek. When cliffs bar our way, we scramble up a talus slope and head into the bush. The waist-deep grasses are still beaded with yesterday's rain and we're instantly soaked. A thick green canopy screens the outside world.

"When did we cross into Brazil?" asks Robert.

"Ow," yells Kirsten. "There are nettles all over the place."

"At least there's one good thing," says Kate, "There aren't any snakes."

We trudge uphill, but the denseness of the undergrowth seems directly proportional to the angle of the slope. We squirm and crawl along alder branches, often not touching the ground for several minutes.

"Uh oh," groans Wendy, "devil's club!"

The broad leaves of the devil's club look innocent, but they screen vicious spikes. I try to make myself thinner. I try to squeeze between the thorny branches, but my clothes aren't armor-plated and I feel sharp stabs of pain.

"There's a clearing ahead," shouts Jody, "but it's covered with nettles."

"Ooh, ooh, oooh!" Piglet squeals of pain from Kirsten. "Ouch! Wendy! Step on that branch." Kirsten is wedged in the foliage, straddling a particularly healthy specimen of devil's club. "Ow, Wendy! Your foot is slipping. Ouch!"

In the worst of the devil's club, we're moving at about a meter per minute. We struggle on, losing heart, but no one wants to be the first to wimp out. We're like small ships bobbing in a sea of brambles, out of sight of land. Scrutinizing the mine site seems less and less important. Finally I realize that we aren't going to make it.

"Are there any fanatics who want to keep going?" I ask. No one answers. Wordlessly we turn downslope and wrestle our way back to camp, every square centimeter of exposed flesh tingling and burning.

Tip-toeing through the devil's club.

Camping in a meadow of paintbrush.

Down at the river we meet the other half of the Tatshenshini Questers who have just arrived. They're lounging under a tarp clutching steaming mugs. We swap stories. Derek tells us about the moose that kept getting caught in a swirling eddy as it tried to ferry across the river. He tells us about Ian's announcement that he was off for a walk and then his immediate retraction, "Well, maybe not," as a blond grizzly lumbered into view.

"What about some tea?" Derek asks.

But we're too itchy from nettles rash and embedded Devil's Club thorns to linger and chat. We return to our camp. Wendy squats beside a stove, primes it, and loses the hairs from the back of her hand in a whoosh of fire. Eventually it settles into a hissing blue flame and she collects a pot of water for bucket baths. Kirsten sits around with a pair of tweezers, plucking thorns. My forearms burn so much from the nettles that I feel nauseous. I lay down in the tent, sweating and dreaming restlessly.

Under the tarp, my friends are talking about Geddes Resources, and their conversation becomes a part of my dream. I imagine ore trucks roaring down a steep incline. I'm mired in devil's club. I can't see the trucks, but I can hear them. I feel the ground shake and choke on the dust. Overhead, helicopters hover like giant predatory insects.

A couple of hours later I wake up feeling weak, but clear-headed. The dreams are gone. I look up and see evening shadows moving across the summits. The only sounds are from the wind in the trees, from the swirling river, and from a chipping sparrow. The black bear is again digging for roots downstream.

It's hard to imagine that, in a couple of years, real dust from rumbling trucks might blow across Tats Creek. I remember reading through Geddes' Revised Stage One Mine Plan during the winter. Their plans seemed fantastic even then. Out here, it all seems like the lurid imagination of a science fiction novelist.

If the proposed mine gets a green light from the B.C. government, giant machinery will move thirty thousand tonnes of ore per day. The eighteen-hundred-meter summit of Windy Craggy Mountain will vanish, becoming instead a gigantic open pit. A mining camp for six hundred workers will spring up in the Tats Creek valley . . . and a mill, and waste dumps, and a hundred-meter high tailings dam. A thirteen-kilometer road and pipeline will link the mine and mill site, ten kilometers of which will cross the active Tats Glacier.

Geddes' first mine plan was rejected in the spring of 1990, largely due to the company failure to develop an adequate plan to deal with acid rock drainage (ARD). ARD occurs when mining exposes sulfur-bearing rock to air and water, producing sulfuric acid. Highly acidic water dissolves heavy metals and becomes deadly for fish. The ore at Windy Craggy has a sulfur content up top six times higher than at other B.C. mines . . . mines already experiencing serious acid problems.

Geddes now proposes to dump non-acid-producing rock on glaciers and sink the rest under the waters of a tailings dam. The company admits that sulfides and carbonates cannot be "simply and directly" correlated with rock types. Acid-base accounting tests have proven unreliable over the years, even in laboratories; there will be no margin for error if waste rock is heaped on glaciers. The revised mine plan says it will confine acidic water "to the greatest degree practical" — hardly a reassuring statement.

Windy Craggy is in Canada's highest-risk earthquake area, just 120 kilometers from the epicenter of the largest earthquake ever recorded in North America. An earthquake could trigger avalanches and landslides that might turn a pipeline into an accordion of twisted metal and cause a catastrophic release of toxic materials. The prospect of a breech in the dam itself, always a possibility, is unthinkable.

Geddes' Revised Stage One Mine Plan is currently stalled somewhere in the bowels of the B.C. government buildings, its fate waiting until the quagmire of B.C. politics is temporarily solidified by a provincial election which by law must occur before the end of 1991. The proposed life span of the mine is at most a couple of decades, but the risk of acid rock drainage would endure for thousands of years.

Two views of the world . . .

Expert assessment has placed this river in the top echelon of wilderness rivers when judged at an international scale of reference.
— Jake Masselink, Assistant Deputy Minister, B.C. Parks

It all comes back to the fact we can't enjoy this planet in a cash economy unless we have the cash to enjoy it with . . .
— Gerald Harper, *Yukon News*, Feb. 28, 1990

July 14-20, 1991

Below Tats Creek, the Tatshenshini becomes wide and braided, swollen with water and gravel from dozens of rushing glacial streams. Soon we round a corner and see a river from the north that makes the Tat look small. The Alsek. After the meeting of the two mighty currents, we float on a sea of moving water that at times is several kilometers wide.

I dip my hand in the Alsek and say to Jody, "This water was slamming through Turnback Canyon not long ago."

"Yeah," he answers with a grin. "that makes this a *way* cooler river."

A couple of hours later we learn first-hand about the exploding popularity of the Tat. On the upper river, I had felt lost in the immensity of the mountains, as though we were the only humans moving through the wilderness. But at the Walker Glacier, rafts drifting in eddies and the colorful splotches of tents attest that this is a bottleneck where every group lingers.

"So much for our wilderness experience," says Sue.

At first I too am disappointed by the traffic and obvious signs of people. But after we shift our camp a few hundred meters downstream, I realize just how small we are — and how big this land is. I walk through dunes to the verge of the glacier's terminal moraine. Moose, grizzly, and wolf prints intertwine with running shoe tracks in the sand.

Many river travellers will speak out in the fight to preserve the Tat. The river needs this constituency more than I need complete solitude. This summer more than a thousand people will float down to Dry Bay. And, unless the mine is developed, its popularity can only increase. The river will need to be managed so that expanding numbers don't trample the wilderness, but such management can be done. The Colorado River, a river that is often compared to the Tat in terms of sheer grandeur, has tens of thousands of visitors annually, but is strictly regulated and well preserved.

In the afternoon we hike to the bottom skirts of the glacier and follow a broad ramp of ice that leads to the base of an ice fall. Deep crevasses and sapphire-colored séracs bar the route to the upper ice fields. An hour from the river we glimpse a world normally inhabited only by mountaineers and mountain goats.

The Walker Glacier.

The next morning a persistent wind from the Pacific moans over the glacier. Low clouds peer over the western mountains and crawl up the Alsek. Rain splutters in fits and starts, eventually settling into a steady drizzle. We fight the temptation to stay in our sleeping bags. We load the boats and launch into a silt-gray river that flows into the clouds.

It's midsummer but it's cold. The raw breeze whips the warmth from our bodies and replaces it with damp chill. Our destination is Alsek Lake, a widening in the river at the terminus of a pair of massive valley glaciers. No one wants to stop until we get there. We paddle steadily, watching hanging glaciers the color of burnished steel slide upriver in the mist. Everyone is layered in rain gear, everyone is withdrawn into their own world.

Eventually I turn the bow of my kayak towards the raft and paddle over. "How are you doing?" I ask.

No one feels like talking, and Kirsten looks miserable. I suggest that we break out a snack, but Wendy says that the food is buried too deep. I take another look at Kirsten's face, and insist that we have something to eat. "How cold are you?" I ask.

"My hands are cold, but I'm okay." There is a time lag in her answer, as though we're speaking at extreme long distance.

I hand over my polypropylene hat and tell her to take off her sodden toque. We pull over on a sand bar and pass around a plastic bag of Smarties. Kirsten is moving in slow motion, numbed by the weather. We cluster around her, pulling and prodding as though she's a mannequin, replacing her wet clothes with dry ones.

"We'll have to camp and warm Kirsten up," I say.

The nearest flat ground is a field thick with vibrant red, orange, and yellow coastal paintbrush. We set up the tents, shove Kirsten into her sleeping bag, and fill her with hot chocolate and soup. As soon as we're sure that she's okay, the rest of us vanish. Our camp becomes a motionless scattering of bright nylon in a monsoon. In the morning though, the monotonous patter stops and thin sunshine pierces the clouds.

We dry out and paddle to Alsek Lake. We collect small chunks of driftwood to bake hot biscuits for lunch. Wisps of smoke drift up from the dutch ovens. Tents spring up. No one talks much. It's partly melancholy from the knowledge that the trip is almost over, partly an unwillingness to speak in what must be one of the most splendid natural cathedrals in the world.

Mt. Fairweather, B.C.'s highest mountain, briefly shows its ghostlike summit through the clouds. The Alsek and Grand Plateau glaciers crawl down from the peaks like monstrous caterpillars, shuddering and roaring as they calve icebergs into the lake. At first we look up each time a boom rolls across the water, but gradually we become attuned. The bass roars become an irregular percussion beat in a symphony of moving water, wind, and bird calls.

While the others explore the shoreline and watch arctic terns, gulls, and jaegers circling over their nests, Jody and I invent a new sport: iceberg jumping. We paddle out to a cluster of bergs blown over from the ice walls. Choosing a likely-looking colossus of ice, we drag our kayaks to its crest, slide down a slippery ramp, and launch like seals into the water.

Later we watch a huge iceberg overturn in a tidal wave of spray. The one we'd played on disintegrates as we're sleeping. Icebergs frequently flip because underwater ice melts faster than the surface exposed to the air, making them top-heavy. Our game was fun, but not prudent.

We pack up and leave the next evening. The glaciers seem remote, falling from the sky like the frozen tears of the mountain gods. We paddle to the outlet of the lake and the swift current whisks us towards salt water.

The throb of a generator signals that we are nearing the Dry Bay fish packing plant. A brown Glacier Bay National Park sign points downriver to the rudimentary campground adjacent to a gravel runway. One of the groups we had seen at the Walker Glacier is already in residence. We set up near a tent city of identical green A-frames.

A web of dirt tracks surrounds Dry Bay. All-terrain vehicles with fish bins circle endlessly. One man has a twenty-four-pack of beer and several bottles of whiskey on his four-wheeler. He weaves over and offers us a drink.

"No thanks," I say. I'm not yet ready to swap the rhythms of river travel for the convenience of a twist top.

"What time is our plane due?" asks Robert. Six of us want to walk to the ocean before the DC-3 picks us up the next afternoon. It is important for us to reach salt water, important for us to see where the Tatshenshini water meets the sea.

Iceberg jumping.

The Tatshenshini wilderness.

"We're scheduled for a late afternoon flight," answers Wendy. "We'd better start hiking by eight o'clock." Our trip isn't quite over, but we're already digging out watches from the depths of waterproof bags and adjusting to schedules. The next morning, for the first time in two weeks, we get up when alarms ring, rather than when our bodies tell us it's time. Robert is already up and gone.

The tidal flats stretch out like prairies. We follow the faint impressions of tire tracks, watching gulls, terns, and bald eagles down by the Alsek estuary. We stoop to pick wild strawberries, sweet red berries tucked in with coastal paintbrush.

"What's that?" asks Wendy, pointing towards the coast.

"It looks like a horse," I say.

Sue whips out her binoculars. "That's no horse, it's a grizzly."

We climb a knoll and watch the bear ambling towards us. A gentle offshore breeze blows our scent the other way, but at three hundred meters, it hears us talking and looks our way. "Don't worry," I whisper. "There has never been a recorded instance of a grizzly attacking a group of six or more."

There's a short pause and then Kirsten says intensely, "There are *five* of us." The bear though, wants no part of us. It lopes off, eating up the ground in powerful strides.

We find Robert on the beach where the Tatshenshini-Alsek meets the ocean. The surf collides with the river current in a series of weird triangular breakers. Foam-flecked water rushes up the sand and tugs at Robert's ankles. Harbor seals bob up, stare at him with round dark eyes, and sink out of sight.

We sit on a log eating crackers and cheese. Robert, Sue, and Wendy discuss whether a small sandpiper is a rufous-necked stint or a sanderling. A juvenile bald eagle flaps lazily overhead. We sit until Jody's watch tells us it's time to go. Turning our backs to the sea, we head reluctantly towards the air strip.

Our trip seems over, but the wilderness isn't quite finished with us. Surrounded by a milling crowd of gulls and terns, a young wolf is feeding placidly on salmon offal. Like the grizzly, it runs off as soon as it sees us. Even frail humans on foot disturb the rhythms of the wild. "But not as much as explosives," I think, "not as much as heavy equipment, not as much as acid rock drainage."

The 1950s vintage DC-3 touches down at Dry Bay on schedule. It's painted green and yellow. The logo of a can-can girl and the words "Lady Lou" are painted on the tail. As we pass our kayaks up to the flight attendants, another raft group carries its gear up from the river. They wander over and we briefly discuss our trips. A couple of them have heard about the Tatshenshini Wilderness Quest. A reporter from *National Geographic* arranges to interview us in Whitehorse in a couple of days.

The civilized face of the Quest turns towards me, the face of the media, of ringing telephones, of paperwork. I'd rather head out on another trip, but this is something I must do. I take a last breath of salt air and another look at the mountains. It'll have to sustain me until September when we'll return to the Alsek and Turnback Canyon. I get on the plane.

CHILKAT RIVER

A TASTE OF SMALL-TOWN POLITICS

March 1990

"I have to warn you. In the past, some meetings like this one have turned ugly."

I tear my eyes away from the picture window where I've been watching a squall race across the Haines harbour, blowing the tops off the whitecaps in Lynn Canal.

"A few years ago," Peter continues, "A Sierra Club bumper sticker was sure to get you a rock through your windshield. Dick Folta, the lawyer who helped start a local conservation group, was run out of town."

I help load the back of Peter's jeep with projector, screen, and slide trays and he drives us through the early evening dusk to the Haines Senior Citizen's Center auditorium. A few boisterous butterflies flutter in my stomach, like an echo of the nervousness I feel when approaching a difficult rapid.

It takes only a few minutes to set out chairs and adjust the projector. A few people drift through the door, carrying plates of homemade cookies and muffins. A coffee percolator burps gently.

"So far," whispers Peter, "so good. It looks like a friendly crowd."

It's an eclectic group, but it's impossible to pigeonhole people by their appearance. Everyone is weathered. There isn't a tie or pair of high heels in sight. Several old-timers immediately stake out chairs and look towards the blank screen, waiting. There are a sprinkling of professionals like Peter, mingling with young people who look as though they've stepped through a time warp from the 1960s. They must be the "Mud Bay hippies."

Someone dims the lights and the first slides glow on the screen. With images of the Tatshenshini and Alsek wilderness in front of me, it's easy to relax and talk about wild country and the proposed mammoth copper mine at Windy Craggy Mountain. I'm low-key about the mine's potential impacts on Haines. I've been warned that some locals would resent a Canadian mouthing off about American issues.

Many folks linger after I'm finished to munch on cookies and chat with their friends. Most people smile, shake my hand, and talk about the beauty of the wilderness, but a few stand stiffly, lips pursed. One old man walks over and points an arthritic finger at me. "It's fine for you kids to want to keep the rivers to yourselves," he says, "but this town needs jobs."

We stack the chairs against the wall and carry the equipment into a drizzling rain. The windshield is intact, but I have an uneasy feeling, as though we're walking along the slopes of what is supposed to be a dormant volcano, while steam rises from the vents and the ground shakes.

The Haines Highway.

April 1991

    I lash my kayak to the roof racks. In mid-April, Yukon rivers are still iced over, but I hope that the Chilkat, bathed by mild air streaming in from the Pacific, will be running. I turn the wheels south at Haines Junction and speed along the Haines Highway that winds from the boreal forest up into the alpine slopes of the Coast Mountains. I catch a glimpse of the upper canyon of the Tatshenshini, a flashing vision of sagging snow bridges with a glint of dark water rushing beneath.

    Near the headwaters of the Tatshenshini, the location of Geddes Resources' proposed access road to Windy Craggy, a white expanse glitters in the sun. If the mine goes ahead, this is where travellers will begin meeting ore trucks — one every ten minutes, twenty-four hours a day. Today the road is empty and I pass just one car in the ninety minutes it takes to get to my launching site on the Chilkat River.

    My kayak has languished on the basement floor since October and I imagine that it shares my pleasure at sliding into moving water. Thick clouds often gloom this valley, but today I squint in the bright light reflecting from glaciers on the verge of the St. Elias Mountains.

    The snow line descends into the forest, a deep green skirt of conifers with a thin hem of deciduous trees nearer the river. In a gnarled cottonwood waiting to burst into leaf, a pair of bald eagles perch above a nest the size of my kitchen table.

Downstream, half a dozen blotchy juveniles and as many boldly patterned adults squat on piles of driftwood. Their heads swivel on motionless bodies, keeping me in view as I drift past.

I grind to a halt on an unoccupied gravel bar and stand up to stretch. Washed up on this beach are the dried husks of spawned-out salmon, grinning rows of jagged teeth and hollow eye sockets. They look just like the graphics on a Mud Bay hippy's T-shirt . . . "Spawn 'til you die."

When September snows chase summer to the south, migratory species and Winnebagos flee the Yukon and Alaska. The motor homes cruise straight to Arizona, but bald eagles head for the Chilkat Valley. The maritime weather at the head of Lynn Canal, North America's longest, deepest fjord, means easy living for eagles. Large numbers of spawning salmon ensure a plentiful food supply. Along the stretch of river that I'm now paddling, up to five thousand bald eagles overwinter, the heaviest concentration in the world.

By the time I beach my boat again, I've paddled eight kilometers and counted thirty-seven bald eagles. And this is the time of year when only the resident birds remain in the Chilkat Valley, one-tenth of the swollen winter population.

I ditch the kayak in the cottonwoods. I trot through the bush to the winding highway and head back towards my car. After a while a rusty pick-up crawls around the corner. I stick out my thumb and it rattles to a stop.

A grey-muzzled golden lab is sitting in the passenger seat. I climb in, hunching my shoulders so I can squeeze between the dog and the door. It sighs heavily in my face and slumps down in my lap.

"Great day, huh?" says the driver, a young man in a plaid shirt and overalls.

"It's fabulous," I answer. "Back in Whitehorse it's still winter."

"Yeah, things are pretty good here now," he says, "and it should stay that way as long as you Canadians don't carve up your toxic mountains and ship them down to us."

In the morning, outside Peter and Linda's window the waters of the Lynn Canal are placid, reflecting mountains that look glossy and unreal. Hardwood floors and the smell of freshly ground coffee don't seem to fit with steep ridges and hanging glaciers.

"Now you know what it's like to live in a picture postcard," says Peter.

Peter Enticknapp is a refugee from the corporate wars of southern California. Like many others, he and Linda found a patch of Utopia in Haines, but just as they began to relax, they discovered the dogs of development still snapping at their heels.

Wearing neat but casual clothes, Peter looks just like what he is, a financial wizard turned small-town real-estate agent. The pro-development burghers of town no doubt prepared to welcome a new ally. How could they know that behind that conservative façade lurked an uncompromising opponent to the proposed Windy Craggy copper mine?

With visions of L.A. smog and endless shopping malls fresh in his mind, Peter could vividly imagine the changes the mega-project might bring to this corner of Alaska if it went ahead . . . millions of liters of fuel and hazardous chemicals rolling through the Chilkat Valley, toxic waste water gushing into Lynn Canal from a proposed pipeline, continuous heavy truck traffic, and a sudden strain on the town's social services from the influx of workers.

Up the stairs is a landing with swivel chairs and a computer — the nerve centre of the Haines fight against the mine. Peter has stirred up a staggering number of people, sent an avalanche of letters, and flown across the continent carrying the message . . . stop the Windy Craggy Mine. Only a few weeks earlier, he and I met at a "Friends of the River" conference in San Francisco, where we handed out brochures, sold T-shirts, and put on a workshop.

The mountains out the window are almost too bright and I look down into the back garden. There's a pile of moose shit plopped on the dregs of winter snow where daffodils will soon be blossoming. Out of the corner of my eye I see a dark shape soaring, silhouetted against the white peaks across the canal. It drifts lower until its body blends with the dark blues of treed slopes and all that is visible are jerky flashes of white head and tail feathers. The eagle sweeps in front of me and disappears to the north, heading for the Chilkat.

The Haines Harbour.

Since my slide show fifteen months ago, there has been a series of town meetings about Windy Craggy, including hotly partisan debates and visits by officials from Geddes Resources. I tell Peter that I'd like to interview some townfolk, to see for myself where the weather vane of public opinion is pointing.

"If you want to talk with a fisherman," says Peter, "try Norm Blank. He lives in a Cape Cod house just down the hill."

Sometime in the night, a young moose had trotted along the dirt road towards town. I follow its prints down a hill and branch off into a driveway bordered by a red wooden fence. A woman kneels in the warm earth around the back, surrounded by splashes of purple and white buds. I knock on the door of the small shingled house, hear an answering shout, and walk into the kitchen.

"Come in," says a white bearded man with cheeks creased by sun and wind. "I'm Norm."

I follow him into a neat, cheerful living room. Crowded by the window are tray after tray of plant pots, with tiny green shoots pushing through the soil. Outside the window is a narrow strip of lawn, a small picket fence, and the road that the trucks from Windy Craggy would roar along if the mine is developed.

He tells me that he moved here thirty-two years ago. Before turning to commercial salmon fishing he wrangled the game warden's job. His first arrest was the local timber boss, John Schnable, for shooting a moose from a boat. Strictly illegal, but Schnable was used to doing things his way. "He kind of ran the town," says Norm.

Those were the days before the Chilkat Eagle Preserve. Conservation and preservation were words you didn't say in polite company . . . but Norm and a few others formed Lynn Canal Conservation, Inc. (LCC).

"LCC endorsed the concept of a preserve," says Norm intently, leaning forward, "just the concept of it, but that was enough to get you run out of town in those days. People's windows were smashed and Dick Folta, the lawyer who helped organize it, had the lug nuts loosened on his car."

By this time, Norm had abandoned his job as game warden and turned to fishing. One Fourth of July weekend, a logger tried to punch him out on Main Street, outside one of the local bars. In the fall, the heavy equipment operators refused to haul his boat out of the water.

"You find out who your friends are," he says with a wry smile.

"Have people changed?" I ask.

"It seems that things aren't so one-sided now," he replies. "People everywhere are more in concert with environmental thoughts. The dinosaurs, the power brokers, they're still around, lamenting at their loss of control . . . but they're slowly becoming extinct."

"What do you think of Windy Craggy?"

He is quiet for a moment, as though he doesn't know where to start. Then he talks about toxic effluent spewing directly into Lynn Canal from a proposed slurry pipeline. He describes disturbance to salmon spawning beds from possible road upgrading. "And," he says, "there are bound to be spills. Heavy metals will leach into the rivers and ocean."

While he's talking I can hear the muted murmer of a pick-up truck outside, cruising towards downtown.

"Yeah," he says. "I'd be able to hear ore trucks carrying Windy Craggy Mountain past my house."

A young woman's voice floats through the door. "Hey, I think the eulachon (smelt) are running."

Norm looks up. "What? Did you hear the birds?"

"Yeah, the gulls and terns were screaming."

He looks at me. "Have you ever seen the eulachon run? When they spawn, the gulls swarm and the sea boils with life. Salmon feed on them, and sea lions and orcas follow the salmon."

For a moment I wish that I was part of this community, that the rhythms of my life could be tuned to the pulse of the ocean. But the moment passes, it's not to be, and I'm content to have shared Norm's insight into the importance of the sea, the unpolluted sea, to the animal and human inhabitants of the Chilkat Valley. I get up from the chair and we shake hands.

"It's so unnecessary," he says in parting. "We're nickle and diming the world to death. It'll be bad for Haines, but even worse for the wilderness up at the Tatshenshini."

Downtown Haines.

Late that afternoon I drive out to Mud Bay to visit Katey and Eric. We had first met several years earlier on a lonely stretch of the Klondike Highway, where encountering another kayak-laden car means instant kinship.

Thick forest shades the trail to their new home and I tread carefully over the icy crust of snow. After four or five minutes of walking, I see an unobtrusive two-story cabin buried in the cedars. I knock and shout, but no one answers. I slip off my soggy running shoes and walk in.

Against the wall is a wooden board crammed with mason jars of spices, dried beans, and peanut butter. The couch is home-made, constructed from thick planks, covered with cushions that don't quite fit, cushions that I later learn have been scrounged from a dumpster. A rickety metal ladder ascends to their bedroom loft.

Soon Katey and Eric emerge from the woods and clatter into the room. Eric fires up a propane two-burner stove and cooks up some tortillas, beans, and rice. The sun disappears into the cedars and a companionable darkness blankets the forest home of my Mud Bay hippy friends.

There is a yell at the door and Scott and Ellen walk into the room, looking like they came straight out of a Tolkienesque fable. Scott, with flowing, reddish-blond hair and a beard that droops to midchest, looks like an overgrown dwarf. Laughter hides behind his John Lennon glasses. Ellen's long dark hair frames eyes that smoulder when she talks. Like the rest of us, she fled from the tsunami of environmental doom breaking over southern Canada and the lower forty-eight states. She is patiently waiting for the world economy to collapse. She just hopes it happens before environmental devastation makes it impossible to live in Alaska off the sea and the land.

I'm comfortable here, sitting on the floor, listening to the soft hiss of the propane lantern. Our conversation is like a butterfly that flits from subject to subject, landing briefly on nuclear waste and dammed rivers, fluttering to subsistence fishing, finally settling on Windy Craggy.

"Remember that first meeting with Geddes Resources?" asks Katey. "When they walked in wearing dark suits and ties and looking like mafiosi? Gerald Harper told them to dress down last time, so they'd be at one with us country hicks."

"You should have seen it," says Ellen to me. "This huge sockeye salmon came swimming into the room and died in agony in front of the stage. When they dragged it out, its silvery costume got ripped."

"I can't wait until the next meeting," says Scott. "We'll sew suits for a whole school of fish."

"Maybe we should send a snowmachine through the room," suggests Eric, "with a big sign saying Chilkat Snowmobilers against Geddes."

Eric slots a cassette into a red ghetto blaster next to a jar of oregano. It's a recording of a local radio show about Windy Craggy's potential impact on Haines. We dip tortilla chips into salsa and listen to monotonous voices apparently trying to lull the moderator to sleep so she won't ask difficult questions. First up is a man from Environment Canada, then the chairman of the B.C. Mine Development Steering Committee, then someone from a Juneau firm that compiled a socio-economic study about Haines and Windy Craggy.

The main act is a debate between two Haines residents. Drew Degan, a composer and pride of Mud Bay, leads off. He talks about potential negative impacts of Windy Craggy and the need to ensure that Haines doesn't lose the things that make it a desirable place to live.

"Yeah," cheers Scott, "hang on to what we got!"

The pro-development speaker is John Schnable. He talks about the flow of dollars that will run from the mine. He mentions a town called Douglas, Arizona, an old mining town that he describes as a beauty spot and tourist attraction.

"He calls it Douglas," laughs Eric. "People down there call it Dog's Ass — it's been so trashed by mining."

The tape drones on. Degan and Schnable each quote the socio-economic report to back up their arguments. We look towards the ghetto blaster as if we're the crowd at All-Star Wrestling, booing the bad guy and cheering when our man gets in a few good licks.

Schnable extolls the importance of logging, but insists that we need Windy Craggy to cushion the loss if the forest industry dies out. He concludes with a plea for Geddes dollars to maintain and improve the infrastructure that has been built up in the town: the arts center, the swimming pool, the library, sidewalks.

"Shit, sidewalks!" says Scott. "God damn."

The tape clicks off and we're convinced that Drew won the debate hands down. The situation is polarized; there is no middle ground. We sit in the Mud Bay darkness feeling like forest guerillas. Environmentalists have lost too many skirmishes already; if we lose the war there'll be nothing much left to fight for.

The next morning I dial Dick Folta's number. A month ago I spent part of a Vancouver morning talking with a $140-per-hour barrister in a black suit. I wonder if a small-town lawyer will make time to talk with me for free.

"Sure," he says, "any time this morning. Just come on in."

I walk down a gravel road to a square gray building on the waterfront that looks more like a small warehouse than a law office. Richard Folta — Attorney, P.C. is inscribed on a wooden plaque colored with dark, mountain-shaped water stains. Inside, a man with graying hair and eyebrows is sliding a ruler over a desk covered with blueprints. He shoves them aside and leans forward to shake hands.

"I saw your slide show last winter," he says.

He leans back in his chair and tells me about the early seventies when Haines was a mill town and Lynn Canal Conservation was a fledgling group. One of its first issues was the establishment of an eagle preserve on the Chilkat.

In the lower forty-eight states, DDT concentrations were causing bald eagle eggs to shatter before the chicks could hatch. The national symbol of the land of the free was an endangered species. In Alaska, if fish stocks remained healthy, then the eagles could take care of themselves. LCC felt that extensive clearcut logging was the main threat to salmon and eagle populations.

The Chilkat Valley became an environmental hot spot. Conservation groups lobbied in Washington, politicians flew to Haines to look at the eagles, and Senator Gary Hart from Colorado proposed a bill to protect their habitat.

"The local bosses would have liked to go back to the good old days when there was a bounty on eagles," says Dick, "but they were smart enough to see where things were headed. So John Schnable about-faced and petitioned for the creation of an Alaska State Preserve on the Chilkat. He knew that the state would be less restrictive than the Feds, and they could keep their influence over logging."

He looks up and away, talking in slow, measured tones, as if all the emotions were wrung out of him during those years. He tells me about smashed windows, about business dropping off, about wheels vibrating with loosened lug nuts.

"It was an ugly time," he says, "even before the phone calls started. They were more than just crank calls. They said they were going to cut up my daughter. I left town in 1980 . . . I couldn't put my kids at risk."

"Could the same sort of thing happen now?" I ask. "Over Windy Craggy?"

"Sometimes the tension seems gone," he continues, "but violence isn't far below the surface." Since he returned to Haines four years ago, Dick tells me, he's noticed a big change. Professionals and artists have moved in, people who have seen environmental horrors in the south, people who have nowhere else to run.

"Red flags went up in town," he says, "when a local fisheries biologist asked Gerald Harper if he could promise that fish wouldn't be affected by Geddes's plans. Harper wouldn't give that guarantee."

I'm shaken as I walk up the hill to Peter and Linda's. I wonder if I'd have the courage to speak out if violence shadowed the path of my convictions.

In the good old days there was a bounty on eagles.

In a recent a poll about Windy Craggy, 69 percent of Haines respondents were opposed to ore trucks rumbling through the Chilkat Valley. Still, there are people who think that the economic benefits would outweigh environmental threats.

There is a fence that runs through Haines, a fence that divides opinion about industrial development. Everyone I've run into has been firmly on the preservationist side, but I've felt the presence of one man, staring through the barbed wire at me. I know that I'll have to climb through the strands of wire and talk with John Schnable before I leave town.

I park outside the Northern Timber Corporation office. My Toyota looks out of place in a line of pickups with big knobby tires. On a graded slope above me are a couple of blue warehouses and a line of derelict, rusting trucks. Around back I can see a duck pond with several decoy mallards and a pair of plastic Canada geese bobbing in the breeze.

Inside, the receptionist is talking on the phone. I stand awkwardly in the foyer until she puts her hand over the mouthpiece and whispers that John Schnable is waiting in an office down the hall. Schnable, wearing Levis and a worker's brown and white checked shirt, is in his seventies. I sit down in a wooden chair below a poster of the Milky Way Galaxy featuring an arrow and the words, "You are here."

"I look at development on a planetary basis," John says in a grandfatherly voice. He tells me that he's been a supporter of Haines for decades, that he and his family built a sawmill that employed many of the men in town, that the Chilkat Valley has prospered because of the forest industry.

"I hate to see trees growing old, falling over, and rotting in the forest," he adds.

"How does Windy Craggy fit into the picture?" I ask.

"You've got to have copper," he says. "Copper pulled us out of the stone age; it pulled us out of savagery. Look, maybe a guy in Iraq might want a VCR. If we can give him the copper wire so he'll have a better view of the world . . . well it's our duty."

Schnable says that he is going to take me back in time, to the days before Haines had a tractor to clear the snow, to the building of the Haines Highway, to the first Alaska ferries to arrive in town. He talks of school improvements, of docks, of libraries, museums, pools, and art centers. He talks of Windy Craggy money.

I've been here for more than an hour already. I squirm in the hard chair and the glare of flickering fluorescent lights. I try to interrupt to ask a question, but I can't deflect the rush of his words once they pick up momentum.

He tells me about lawsuits that the Sierra Club and the Audubon Society filed against his logging practices. I hear that marketable timber in the Tongass National Forest is rotting because they won't let him cut it, that the preservationists don't want a single tree felled or a stone turned over. I hear that the LCC were out to get him through the eagle preserve wrangle.

Bald eagles nesting along the Chilkat.

"They didn't really care about the eagles," he says. "I personally take credit for that eagle preserve. The Feds would have shut down the whole valley if we hadn't compromised."

From Haines we embark on a journey of words to Bisbee, Arizona, the home of the Dodge Copper Mine. Schnable describes its beauty, the historic underground workings, the flowers and nice ponds. He says that there was no damage, unless I wanted to call a hole in the ground degradation.

"There's no doubt that the Windy Craggy mine would be a tourist attraction," he says. "I've walked down the Tatshenshini — now it's nothing but buckbrush, mosquitoes, and misery. But tourists will drive their Winnebagos over the most difficult roads to see old mines."

"I've heard that things have been pretty rough between you guys and the LCC," I comment, "and that Dick Folta was run out of town."

"This is the same shit that I've heard for years," he answers with a hard edge to his voice. "Dick Folta was never treated by anybody with disrespect. Oh, I've heard stories about his loosened lug nuts and stories about threats. He's not telling the truth. I never showed Mr. Folta anything but courtesy. We've always believed that Dick Folta was on the payroll of the Sierra Club. And people like Norm Blank used to come forward at every meeting talking about the damn fish. According to him, fishing is the only thing . . . he believes what he says, that's the oddity of it."

"I have one last question," I say, "It seems that more and more people are fighting things like Windy Craggy. How has the town changed over the years?"

"I'm disappointed," he answers. "People used to admire the work ethic."

He leans forward, puts his elbows on the table, and says that he is going to tell me his vision of the future. The population of the world will grow to eleven billion by 2010, because sex will be here until the last wiggle — and those people are going to need cars — electric cars. We'll drill holes through the earth's crust to tap geothermal energy for power. We'll need to string transmission lines all over the continent and manufacture millions of batteries. We'll need tons of copper.

"Windy Craggy will help us replace the internal combustion engine," he says. "It will be good for the environment."

I walk into the salt breeze blowing off the Chilkat Estuary and rub the fluorescent glare from my eyes. While it was interesting to hear such a different view of the world, I would rather have been floating down the river. If Windy Craggy is developed, I wonder whether the fish and eagles on the Chilkat, and the Dall sheep and grizzlies on the Tatshenshini, will understand that the trucks roaring by and the acid mine run-off are actually good for their environment.

May 1991

Seven canoes, a sea kayak, and a couple of rafts buzz back and forth in the eddy, like giant water beetles. On shore, people are carrying more rafts and milling around. We don't have any champagne, so Jody opens a beer and dribbles it over Derek's kayak. The Tatshenshini Wilderness Quest is launched.

Derek, Ian, Jody, and I had dreamed up the Quest during the pit of December, when paddling in any form sounded good. Winter has now melted away. Other summertime adventures beckon, but our dream still feels right. The Chilkat is the first of the three rivers that we'll paddle, rivers threatened by the Windy Craggy project.

Launching the Tatshenshini Wilderness Quest.

The Chilkat paddle will be an afternoon float, a mild beginning to a project that will continue on the Tatshenshini in July, and culminate on the turbulent waters of the Alsek in September.

While we're organizing gear, Peter Johnson, the vice-chief of the Chilkoot Indians, drives up and gets out of his car. We edge close so we can hear his quiet voice. He tells us that the Chilkoots are opposed to the mine, that fish and eagles are more important than Windy Craggy. "I can't come with you today," he says, "but I wanted you to know that my people support what you are doing."

Tracee wanders to the river carrying three-month-old Adam, who is engulfed by his life jacket. Kids of assorted sizes are throwing sticks into the water and scrambling over gunnels into canoes. My daughter Polly and two of her teenage friends clamber into a raft with some university students from Saskatchewan.

The president of LCC, Tom Ely, paddles upriver in a sleek sea kayak. A director of Friends of the Earth and another from the Yukon Conservation Society sit together in a borrowed canoe, looking nervously at the moving water. The Southeast Alaska Conservation Council is represented, as well as the Canadian Parks and Wilderness Society, and Friends of Yukon Rivers. Usually, northern environmental groups meet only in stuffy strategy sessions. Today we will taste the crisp salt breeze and feel splashes of cold water on our arms.

"Zoë ... come," yells Keith. A black puppy bounds through a thicket of legs and jumps into the canoe.

"Hey Ken," says Jody. "There are fifty-nine people here, not counting the little kids and the dog."

I normally paddle with small groups of friends, but this is an armada, an armada armed with hopes and determination. We float in the gentle current, watching light and shadows play on mountains scored by spring avalanches. There is little talk about Windy Craggy. For today, it is enough to be here, sponging up the inspiration that a wild river gives, recharging our batteries.

The end of May is the height of the nesting season for Chilkat River bald eagles. We don't want to disturb them, so we've chosen a stretch of the river without active nesting sites. I haven't seen a single eagle by the time we finish our paddle near the Haines Road.

The shuttle drivers retrieve the cars and we wave goodbye to our friends from Haines. As I tie a final half-hitch to the rope holding four kayaks on the Sagwagon, I see the broad wing span of a bald eagle sweeping over the Chilkat. It descends with heavy wing beats, talons outstretched for landing, and disappears behind the bright new leaves on the cottonwoods.

The eagle makes me think of salmon, of ore trucks, of grizzlies, of the possibility of D-9's gouging a road through the wilderness. It makes me remember why I'm here.

Floating down the Chilkat River.

THE HESS RIVER

ONE CENTURY APART

This is the story of two trips on the Hess River. The first, during the years 1898-99, was an accident.

The Klondike. Lust for gold. There was something about it... something about it that prompted otherwise normal, respectable people to abandon creature comforts and head into the wilderness. And this was a time when wilderness was something to shun, not approach; something to loathe, not love; something to push back, not preserve.

Most Klondike stampeders travelled by ship to Skagway, Alaska. They hauled their outfits up and over the Chilkoot Trail and built ramshackle boats when they reached Lindeman Lake. Then they paddled down the Yukon River to Dawson City.

Edmonton merchants were dismayed at the money gold seekers were spending in Seattle, Vancouver, and Skagway. They felt that they too, deserved a piece of the action and so they championed the "All Canadian Route" to the Klondike.

The October 7, 1897 issue of *The Edmonton Bulletin* printed an article extolling this alternate access to Dawson. The newspaper stated that a prospector *"cannot be cornered and the trail cannot be blocked. It is merely a question of time, particularly the latter. That the route is long and difficult everyone will admit—as are all routes that have been used... The man who has not the resolution and ambition and energy and good management and capital enough to carry him to the Yukon by the Edmonton route will be a great deal better off somewhere else."*

No one could deny the truth in these words.

Ernest J. Corp, from Hamilton, Ontario read the Edmonton newspapers. In his memoirs, *The Trail of '98 by the All Canadian Route*, Corp wrote:

While the vast majority of the thousands heading for the Klondyke went in by way of the Pacific Coast, some hundreds decided to go in by way of Edmonton, over what was called the "All Canadian Route." This was the result of articles published, quoting extracts from a pamphlet by the late Wm. Ogilvie "a then well-known Government Geologist and surveyor," who had described a trip taken by his survey party from Edmonton to Dawson, via the rivers and lakes of the great North West Territories, then down the Mackenzie River to Fort McPherson, up the Peel and Rat Rivers, over a low divide to the head of the Porcupine River, down the Porcupine to the Yukon River at Fort Yukon, and up the Yukon to Dawson. This was a practical route for a party such as his, travelling with light canoes and obtaining needed supplies at the various Hudson Bay Company Posts along the way, but for men headed for the goldfields, dragging along their entire outfit, some having as much as a ton apiece, it was a horse of a different colour.

But then, what greenhorn was going to let a little thing like that bother him?

Spring 1898

Corp is reticent about what drove him to leave home for the Klondike, merely stating that "circumstances had created in me a desire for a change and travel..."

... one day calling on a friend of mine, Jack Phillips (who had a thriving merchant tailor business on James Street), I said, "What do you say we go to the Klondyke?" After a few moments' thought he said, "All right, I'll go if you will."

So we got up a party of six together, and during the following weeks we outfitted for the trail. Our party consisted, besides Phillips and myself, of Dr. Dillabough Jr., Chas. Krugg, Vic McFarland and Alf Willis.

We bought most of our outfit from the local wholesale houses, excepting flour and rolled oats, which we bought later in Edmonton (as it had probably come from around there). At the time aluminum utensils were but little used, and, wanting to avoid unnecessary weight when packing on the portages, two of us went to Buffalo, N.Y. and bought a complete outfit of cooking utensils, all aluminum.

Our heavy winter clothing, sleeping bags and oilskin clothes were all made in Phillips' tailor shop, and when we were ready to start we had as complete an outfit as could be secured for such a trip.

July 1987

Ninety years later, our party of four prepares for a trip on the Hess River. Packing should be easy, after dozens of trips, but it's always a chore. What would it have been like for Corp, in Hamilton, almost a century ago?

Corp packed for a journey that would include overwintering along the way; we would be gone less than a month. Corp adapted nineteenth-century household goods; we buy designer gear for outdoor use — lightweight, compact, and in all the colors of the rainbow.

Our group consists of Wendy Boothroyd, Rachel Shephard, Graham Wilson, and I. Graham squats next to a canoe in the backyard, plastering duct tape over rips in the spray covers while the rest of us pack food.

"How many cups of granola should we bring?" I ask.

"Half a cup per person per day." says Rachel.

"Are you serious? I'll starve."

"I must have quantities written down somewhere," says Wendy. She shuffles through a tattered pile of papers, notes from previous trips.

I do some mental arithmetic. "I'll pack three-quarters of a cup each... so if you only want half a cup, then I get a whole cup."

"No way," says Rachel, "if you're eating three quarters of a cup, I want equal shares."

The kitchen table is covered with flour, dried fruit, chocolate, pasta, and dried refried beans. Plastic bags, filled and unfilled, litter the floor and sprawl around the corner onto the green shag rug in the living room.

"We better test the chocolate," says Rachel, "in case it's going bad."

The green shag is also covered with mounds of clothes, books, sleeping bags, pots, and maps. I search the piles to make sure that the compass is in, then pencil a tick on my notepad. The paper is a scrawl of notes, words crossed out, words with stars. Sun screen isn't starred or ticked, but I'm sure I already threw it in. I dig into another heap to make sure.

My method of packing is time-consuming and clumsy, but reassuring. Each time I pick my way through the living room I have the impression of faint, but steady progress.

"Do you really need all this climbing gear?" asks Wendy.

Underneath the potted avocado tree, aptly named Ugly, there is a heap of ropes, slings, carabiners, and ice axes. Graham, Rachel, and I want to climb Keele Peak, but we don't know what the north side of the mountain will be like. The pile of gear will only be useful if we find a non-technical route.

Graham looks bleary when we drive the Sagwagon to pick him up. He prefers to pack at the last minute, saving time but telescoping the stress into a last-night frenzy. He usually doesn't forget anything essential, maybe just a spoon, or a knife, or powdered milk for coffee. We circle to Brenda Carson's place. She has agreed to drive the Sagwagon back from Sheldon Lake, and pick us up in Mayo at the end of our trip.

"I'll get in the back," says Graham sleepily. The rest of us squeeze into the crew cab.

Constant drizzle at Sheldon Lake.

Summer 1898

Just about that time there was a rate war on between the C.P.R. and the Grand Trunk Railway, and our tickets to Edmonton cost us only twenty-five dollars . . .

Arriving at Edmonton, we found it a small prairie town, with one main street north of the Saskatchewan River . . .

We got our outfit freighted across the river, and pitched our tents in a cottonwood grove in what is now near the heart of the city. We camped here about a week, then arranged to have our whole outfit freighted to Athabasca Landing over the old H.B.C. road, being about seventy-five miles. The freighter made two trips to take our six tons of freight. Arrived here, we made our camp, and started to get our boat ready. It had been made for us in Hamilton by an old boat builder, and had a rock elm keel and ribs, and Georgia pine planking, each part marked and knocked down, which made it easy to reassemble. This, I think, was the strongest boat built here; the scores of other boats were constructed of fresh sawn local lumber, and were just flat bottom scows.

August 1987

We drive all day, rattling north on the Klondike Highway to Carmacks, then east along the Robert Campbell Highway. Ore trucks from the lead-zinc mine at Faro roar south towards the port at Skagway. The trucks look like mythical beasts, two glowing eyes and a green snout in a cloud of smoke. I slow the truck and we are buffeted by the wind, showered by rocks and gravel. There's a sharp crack and a starburst blossoms on the windshield.

"Shit," says Wendy.

I take my foot off the clutch and we lurch forward into the dust.

We camp outside Ross River and in the morning drive into town to telephone Danny Perrault, our pilot. I walk to a pay phone followed by a skinny dog, the only moving thing in sight except two ravens pecking at a plastic bag. I turn around and the dog skitters away, running sideways, its body curled and its tail between its legs.

"I'll meet you at the hotel for coffee," says Danny.

We edge past three men in baseball caps smoking at an arborite table and walk to the self-serve counter. There are no cinnamon buns and I don't like the look of the pies. The blueberry is too brightly colored, squashed down by a tight film of plastic wrap. "Just coffee," I say.

Danny Perrault walks in. He looks cheerful, his face lean and wrinkled by the sun. "Morning," he says and we talk for a few minutes. Then he looks at his watch. "It'll take you a couple of hours to get to Sheldon Lake. I'll meet you there about noon."

We drive onto what looks like a floating wooden dock. Some gears rattle and the ferry twitches along a cable that stretches over the Pelly River. Light rain mists the windshield as we lurch onto the North Canol Road.

The U.S. army dreamed up the Canol Road project during World War II. A pipeline was planned, a pipeline to pump oil from Norman Wells in case the Japanese invaded Alaska. They didn't, the project was abandoned, and derelict U.S. military trucks rust along the gravel shoulders of the North Canol.

The road winds and turns, slides over a hill, winds and turns like a roller coaster. The cloud ceiling lowers and mist covers the heads of the mountains like wool toques. It starts raining in earnest. The rear wheels churn up the road and soon a film of mud oozes across the window of the canopy. I accelerate around a corner, into a sharp dip, and up a steep rise.

"I think I'm going to throw up," says Rachel.

"I feel lousy too," agrees Wendy.

I pump the brakes, and the truck begins to fishtail. I wrestle with the wheel. We slither to a stop. I get out, lose my feet, and grab onto the door's rear-view mirror. The road surface, partly clay, is greasy with rain. Rachel hunches over in the bushes. Wendy breathes deeply, eyes closed.

We're late pulling into Sheldon Lake, but Dànny Perrault isn't here yet. The Ross River ferry only runs until five o'clock, and Brenda is anxious to start driving. We untie the canoes and dump the gear near the lake. She revs the engine and rattles up the road.

The mosquitoes find us. I know that if I walk quickly they will stay behind, like the cloud of dust behind an ore truck. Keeping just ahead of the bugs and listening for the buzzing of Danny's Cessna 185, I beat a path up and down the Canol Road. When I slow down, the mosquitoes billow forward and settle on my head and shoulders. I run back to the lake, where Graham's tent is up and the others are reading, sheltered from the drizzle and the mosquitoes. Wendy squashes her face against the insect netting. "Are the clouds any higher?" she asks.

"Not really," I say, unzipping the fly.

"What about some backgammon?" asks Graham.

"Sure," I answer and we while away the afternoon desultorily tossing dice and shuffling pieces. And the evening. And the next day. And the next morning. Until at last there is a break in the uniform bowl of clouds and the buzz of the float plane drowns out the whine of mosquitoes.

A bunch of Klondike stampeders. Photo courtesy Public Archives of Canada.

Summer 1898

Like many Klondike stampeders, Corp had little experience in wilderness travel, none on rivers. In his narrative however, he wrote of no hesitation, no fears, as he and his companions launched their stout boat into moving water. The first stage of their journey was down the Athabasca River to Lake Athabasca and Fort Chipewyan.

Thinking it was the intention to run all night, when it got dark we hoisted a hurricane lantern to the mast top, and all turned in and went to sleep, leaving the boat to drift on its own, which none of us would have thought of doing after some experience of what rivers are like. My own idea of a river was somewhat like a canal with nice banks, instead of what many are — real death traps, especially under a cut bank with overhanging sweepers which could easily overturn a boat. This was certainly a case of "Ignorance is bliss."

Continuing our journey, we came next to what is called the cascade. This is caused by a rim of rock stretching across the river, over which the water flows as over a dam, the drop being from six to nine feet according to the water... Here again we came very near to losing the big scow of our party, and all its contents. A loaded boat going down the river is brought to the bank, a strong stern line attached and held on to by several men, and lowered slowly toward the cascade, while a light line is attached to the bow of the boat, with one or two men to hold it. The guide, getting on board, called out, "All right, let her come!" . . . we let go of the stern line. The boat immediately swung out, and we heard the guide say, "My God, they have let us go . . .!" The boat swung around in an arc, and was hanging half over the falls . . .

Luckily there were lots of men waiting here, and they jumped into the boat at the risk of their lives and unloaded about eight tons in as many minutes. The empty boat was then dropped over the falls, hauled out, and, with the help of a Spanish windlass, pulled back into shape, and was ready to proceed after a little patching and caulking.

Leaving Chipewyan, our route lay across the end of the lake, where a short river named the La Roche is found. This river, where it joins the mouth of the Peace, forms the Slave River, which runs into Great Slave Lake. The country between the Athabasca Lake and the mouth of the Peace River is practically flat, so that the waters of the Peace River coming from the south get to flood levels before the lake has risen, causing the slow running La Roche River to reverse its flow and go back into the lake for a day or two.

We had been told this by our guide and when the reverse flow started we got out and tracked our boat downstream to the junction of the Peace. Another party who were a few hours behind us happened to tie up for the night just before the reverse flow started. Next morning, starting out, they appeared to be going back upstream, and had quite an argument about it. Not knowing of this peculiarity of the river, they thought they were dreaming, so pulled ashore to figure out what was wrong. Soon another party came along and explained things, to their great relief.

Here at the mouth of the Peace River we came in contact with quite a number of men who had left Edmonton in the fall of '97 to go overland to the Klondyke from there, some of whom we knew from Hamilton. It appears that the thrifty, wide-awake business men and storekeepers of Edmonton had hired a gang of men to cut a trail from Edmonton about fifty miles out into the country, supposedly in the direction of the Yukon, with a dead end, and called it the overland trail to Yukon. Many outfits started out with pack horses, or sleds, but few made it through, more turned back. I was told by several men who followed it through the winter that in the Swan Hills dead horses by the score lay across the trail. Those who got through to the Peace River, after a hard winter's trip, built boats and came down the river, where we met them.

It has been estimated that up to seven hundred people left Edmonton in 1898. They battled north singly, in small groups, and in large throngs. The harsh environment took a toll. Friends became enemies and new alliances formed. Some turned back, some drowned, but many, including Ernest J. Corp, pressed resolutely on. Down the powerful Slave River. Across storm-lashed Great Slave Lake. Into the Mackenzie.

Our next stop was Fort Simpson, the Hudson Bay Company post where the Chief Factor, Mr. Campbell, lived. This post is on a high gravel bank at the mouth of the Liard River. At this point, another party of gold seekers were ready to start up the Liard River, consisting of several strapping young fellows and one old prospector who said he came along to show the young fellows how to do it. I'll always remember seeing them starting up the river, the young fellows on the tracking line and the old man on the boat handling the sweep and calling out in his shaky old voice, "Good-bye, boys, it's only the old timers will get through!"

The upper reaches of the Liard River are very tough going, and I heard later from others who went that way that this party broke up, and the old man left his bones up there.

Here at Simpson we first heard of the Gravel River, flowing into the Mackenzie from the West about two hundred miles further down, where the Indians who travelled up and down it hunting said there was plenty of gold along the gravel bars, and also that over the divide at the head was the Yukon watershed. This story was corroborated by the Factor. After talking it over, we decided to leave the Mackenzie River and go up this river (instead of going on down to the Peel River which had been our original plan), prospect along the bars, and eventually cross over the divide to the Yukon and down to Dawson . . .

Leaving Fort Simpson, we next passed Fort Wrigley, and came to the mouth of the Gravel River, about twenty-five miles above Fort Norman.

We found that this river was well-named the Gravel River, being broken up in many places into several channels flowing between gravel bars and islands, in places miles wide, between its main banks, as far as the eye could see. Just why this very appropriate natural name "Gravel River" has now on the present maps been changed to "Keele River" is hard to understand, but then officialdom often changes a natural name for an arbitrary one.

August 1987

We drone over the broad U-shaped valley of the upper Hess. Danny Perrault points to an olive green lake perched in a narrow plateau. "Porter Puddle," he says laconically.

A moose standing knee deep in a swamp looks up as we flash overhead. We land smoothly and nudge the willow-strewn shore. I crawl onto the pontoon and Wendy hands me gear while Danny unties the canoe.

The plane has ferried us over the Selwyn Mountains and the headwaters of the MacMillan and Hess rivers, 150 kilometers in fifty minutes, 150 kilometers that would have taken Corp months to travel. Danny guns the engines and lifts off to pick up Graham and Rachel, who are still killing time at Sheldon Lake. We dump the gear in a clearing and walk to the top of a rise.

The mountains look old and weathered, gently rounded with smooth transitions between the greens of plant cover and the rusty browns of rock and scree slopes.

Danny Perrault and his Cessna 185.

Bright cumulus clouds rise over the western ramparts of the valley, swiftly becoming dark gray, with ragged undersides, like sheep waiting to be sheared. We run down to the clearing, put on rain jackets, and tip the canoe over the packs.

The shower is heavy. The raindrops hit Porter Puddle so hard that they send splashes upward, as though the drops are trying to leap out of the lake. A northern phalarope wades back and forth in the shallows, then swims across the lake, like a tiny gull.

Wendy shouts, "Ken, look at this crap." She is standing, looking disgusted, next to a pile of rusting cans, rotting cardboard, smashed beer bottles, and an intact Gilby's Gin bottle. Only a few canoeists have paddled the Hess, friends from Whitehorse. They wouldn't willingly leave behind even a twist-tie.

"Must have been prospectors or hunters," says Wendy.

We dig out our plastic garbage bags, brought along for water-proofing, calculating how many we can afford to use. We squish the trash into three bulging bags, brown shards of broken glass poking out. When Danny returns with Graham and Rachel, we gingerly pass him the garbage to take back to civilization.

The portage to the river is through dense willows. I stagger under a canoe, my shoulders bruised by the paddles lashed to the thwarts, the tough roots and branches of the willows grabbing at my feet. Wendy walks past, but all I can see are a pair of light hikers and blue cotton pants.

"Head right at the clearing," she says, "and you'll see where I dropped my pack."

I lurch over to the pile of gear. In films, I've seen frail-looking old men casually shouldering a canoe, and in one fluid motion, flipping it to their knees and gently to the ground. Every time I've tried, it feels like I'm throwing out my back along with the canoe. I lean forward and the bow teeters to the ground. I wait, like a turtle on its back. In a few moments, Rachel comes along and laughs.

"Rachel," I say, "would you grab this bloody boat?" She comes up behind me and steadies the canoe so I can escape. We walk back together for another load.

Here above tree line, the Hess is a brook snaking through the bushes. We load the canoes carelessly, not worried about whitewater yet. Unlike the people who streamed north from Edmonton almost a century ago, the four of us are capable in the wilderness, and on fast-flowing water. Instead of concentrating on survival, we paddle through the Selwyn Valley, free to listen to the breeze tossing in the willows, free to watch the shadows move across the alpine, free to shed civilized worries.

Near the headwaters of the Hess.

The metamorphosis from jumpy urbanite to relaxed backcountry traveller happens slowly. It takes days for me to shed my time sensitivity. We have more than three weeks on a river we could paddle in ten days. My rhythms start to adjust to the daylight, to the land, away from schedules, away from clocks.

Summer 1898 - Winter 1899

The Dawson-bound group now headed upriver, towards the continental divide. It didn't take many days of arduous tracking and portaging to disenchant some of the would-be miners slogging up the Gravel River. But it took more than a little hard work to discourage hardier types like E. J. Corp. It is little wonder that he was christened Ernest.

... two of us crossed over in the dinghy and stood ready to catch the bow line. The bowman threw the rope, but unfortunately for him he dropped a coil, which caught around his ankle. We caught the end of the line and held on, but he, poor fellow, was dragged into the water as the boat swung away from the bank. Unable to release himself, he held on desperately to the rope with both hands, but instantly went out of sight for a moment. Coming to the surface, he yelled, "Hold her boys!" and then again disappeared. Coming to the surface again, the same frantic yell was repeated, "Hold her, boys!" By this time we had managed to drag man and boat to the bank and hauled him aboard. As soon as he got his breath he grinned and said, "Oh, I know it must have appeared funny, but I was afraid you would let go of the rope, and then I would surely have drowned."

Well, we spent the remainder of the summer hauling our big scows upstream, until the cold weather caused the ice to begin running, when we decided to build cabins and wait until the ice was strong enough to travel on. We reckoned we were up over a hundred miles from the Mackenzie ...

My party camped at the mouth of a small creek, with plenty of good timber. We built a large cabin, 15 feet by 30 feet. The other Hamilton party we had been travelling with built cabins across the river on an island. Later two of them came over to visit us on the first ice, and spent the night with us. During the night an ice jamb occurred lower down, backing up the water several feet, and our visitors had to stay until the jamb broke two days later. I decided to go with them, and see how their mates had fared during the high water.

When we got to the island, a desolate scene met our eyes. The island was covered by huge blocks of ice stranded when the jamb broke, and their large wood pile had floated away, but the cabin still stood. It had been flooded half way to the top, and they had piled their goods on the upper bunks and cut a hole in the roof to climb out of should it become necessary. Fortunately, however, the water had receded before reaching the roof.

Corp's narrative is surprisingly light-hearted, considering that he had blundered into the northern boreal forest with winter approaching. He saw humor, even in dangerous situations. He felt fit and healthy. He doesn't mention loneliness, or injury, or death.

Other books about the All Canadian Route are more realistic, but it is difficult to accurately assess the toll exacted by the severe conditions. Charles Geilds, of New York, froze to death after a hard pull through an area of overflow. He was swathed in blankets and placed on a scaffold, since no one could dig a grave in the frozen earth. Many men suffered from scurvy, and at least two more perished.

Back in Edmonton, it was reported that ten men lost their lives along the Gravel. Since some of the named dead later turned up in Dawson, this was obviously inaccurate.

Seemingly oblivious to the hardship, Corp continues on his resolute way.

We started our winter sleighing trip three days before Christmas, 1898, and put in the whole winter relaying our outfits to the continental divide and down into the Yukon watershed.

We all carried extra socks and moccasins on the sled, as quite often in an overflow our feet would get wet and dry footwear was essential to prevent frozen toes. The sleds, having no shoeing, and being made from green lumber, often got roughened up, which made them very hard to pull. One day, by accident, we found out how to remedy this, by turning the sled over and icing the runners by a quick swipe with a wet cloth when we came by an open water hole. However, this was too haphazard, and we made a practice of taking a can of hot water along, well wrapped up, on the sled. One day I met a little Irishman, Johnny O'Hara, on the trail. I said to him, "how is the sled going to-day?" He replied, "Well, Ernie, I'll tell you. It was pulling like a cat by the tail. I kicked it, cussed it, and turned it up and peed on it, and it ran beautifully!" So he, too, had discovered the water cure.

As the weeks passed by, our supplies were gradually getting lighter, and we could move the entire outfit in three loads, two trips with about 300 to 400 pounds each, and one for the camp out-fit — tent, bedding, stove, etc. At noon we often had our lunch on the open river, where we built a fire and boiled water for tea or coffee. One day it was forty below zero, and a fair breeze blowing and the coffee pot sitting at the edge of the fire with steam coming out of the spout, when I noticed a small icicle about an inch long hanging from the spout lip. I drew the attention of the others to it, and they said if they hadn't seen it with their own eyes they would not have believed it could happen.

August 1987

The Klondike stampeders hoped for an easy passage to wealth. Instead they stumbled into the adventure of their lives, an adventure with grim consequences for mistakes — where the wrong choice of foods could mean scurvy, where splashing into an overflow could mean frostbite and amputated toes, where ignorance about sweepers could mean drowning.

Living in North America in the latter part of the twentieth century, it's all too easy to avoid the cold, the wet, the hunger, the danger . . . and also the excitement that comes with adventure. You can acquire a bellyful of vicarious thrills without straying from the television and VCR. The only dangers are being cut by a pop top, or slowly petrifying through lethargy.

Keele Peak.

Some deliberately court danger and hardship . . . leaping off cliffs with paragliders, or squeezing into kayaks above class V rapids, or climbing sheer rock faces. Unlike Corp though, they can plan their adrenaline rushes, and be home in time for a cold beer and a hot shower.

Our three-day paddle through the Selwyn Valley is a beeline towards Keele Peak, but we've seen nothing but a boiling mass of clouds where the mountain should be. One evening the curtain of mist parts for a few minutes and we see its north face, steep, with a huge hanging glacier. The east ridge looks possible, although the approaches to it are hidden by red humps of alpine between us and the summit pyramid.

Hiking above the Hess.

On the map it looks easy — a couple of centimeters of emerald green forest and scattered contour lines. After we've skipped up to the head of a creek, we simply walk across a ridge, and up to the summit. No doubt we'll have time to snap a few photographs before strolling back for a cup of tea.

But my legs start to quiver after only a little bushwhacking. They must have atrophied from paddling all summer. The pack is heavy and the straps dig into my shoulders and the ice axe snags on branches. It takes until dusk to climb to the base of the alpine. It's not as high up the valley as planned, but at least we're above tree line. We call it our base camp and go to sleep.

There's no sun on the tent when I wake up, but it's too bright out. "Damn," I think, "I've overslept." I crawl out to put the water on for coffee. A ground squirrel bounds into the willows and a pair of mountain caribou are silhouetted on the western skyline, but there is no movement from Graham and Rachel's tent.

No one feels like shifting camp, so we decide to do a reconnaissance. We'll hump our climbing gear to the high point of the ridge that encircles the valley like the tiered seats of a Roman amphitheatre. Then, we'll be in position for a lightning ascent the next day.

By the time we walk up the valley and traverse to a col, the usual afternoon weather has come steaming up from the valleys and the muttering of thunder echoes from the Rogue Range on the other side of the Hess. We split up: Graham wanders off to the east, Wendy lingers in the meadows with a flower book, and Rachel and I climb higher, scrambling across the rotten rock at the crest of the ridge.

The clouds thicken, but it doesn't rain. Instead, compact pellets somewhere between hail and snow pepper us. On the red ridges that are now below us, a thin white carpet highlights a network of caribou trails that look like the wrinkles on the back of my grandmother's hands. Finally we clamber high enough to see the approaches to Keele Peak. Between us and the summit pyramid, there is a tortuous mile of knife-edged ridges. Just getting to the base of the mountain would take days of technical rope-work, even if the weather cooperated.

Back at camp, we rationalize our feelings.

"Does it really matter if we climb Keele Peak?"

"I'm happy just being here."

"Yeah, let's hang out for a day or two and explore."

In the morning I wake up feeling rested, but it's still dark and gloomy. The tent sags drunkenly. I punch the walls and feel a glutinous layer of wet snow slide to the ground.

"Just another August day in the Yukon," Wendy says cheerfully.

The clouds dissipate as we scurry back to the river. We bathe and dry off in the sunshine.

Summer 1898

Just to show what greenhorns we were about cooking, I mention this incident. One day while camped at Edmonton, we had a piece of bacon cooking, when someone of our party suggested that, as bacon and beans would soon be our main diet, we try some now. So I put a large cup of beans into the boiling pot, thinking that they would be soft and ready to eat by suppertime, but after many hours of cooking they were still like bullets from being put into boiling water instead of cold. Another man made a plum duff and put it in cold water on the stove, so you can imagine the result . . .

Moving all the time gave us little opportunity to make yeast bread, and continuous baking powder biscuits were hard on the stomach, but yeast pancakes were just the thing.

In the morning at breakfast time I set a large batter of yeast in a dishpan with a top, covered it up in the bed, and cooked a pot of rice and set it on the back of the stove. When we came in at noon for lunch, I dumped the still warm rice into the yeast batter and covered it up again. When we came back again for supper, this mixture would be light and foamy. After supper I would set to with two or three frying pans, making pancakes on top of the box stove. After three or four hours, I would have a pile of pancakes eighteen inches high, enough for two weeks, which, when frozen, were handy to pack and easily thawed out, and very healthy and palatable.

August 1987

Yeasted bread is always welcome, even if you're only out for a couple of weeks. I prove the yeast in a little warm water, rinse the sand off the overturned canoe, and start kneading. I put the dough in the tent which is warm from sunlight.

I wriggle into the sand and lean against a canoe with the book *Texas*, by James Michener. I should have been more careful with my literature selection. Reading about filthy rich Texans while I'm travelling in the wilderness is wearying, but it's the only book I have. I rip out thirty pages of what I've read, crumple it, and hold a lighter to it.

"It's the only thing this book is good for," I mutter to Rachel, feeding twigs to the fire. I need a bed of glowing coals for the dutch oven. Rachel kneels over the blade of a paddle, rolling out tortillas with a water bottle. Dried onions are rehydrating in a pot of hot water, refried beans in a plastic peanut butter jar.

"We'll be paddling big whitewater tomorrow, right?" asks Rachel.

"Yeah."

"Seriously then," she says, "we'd better eat some chocolate in case somebody flips."

"That would be the worst," agrees Wendy, hovering over the Fruit'n'Nut bar with a Swiss Army knife. "We get two and a half squares each."

Kneading bread.

Spring-Summer 1899

The stampeders who trudged up the Gravel River were hoping to slip into the headwaters of the South MacMillan. I take a few moments from the word processor to spread topo maps on the rug. It is easy to see where they went wrong. The water that trickles into a tributary of the Hess is only a few kilometers from the top of the MacMillan watershed.

> When we reached the continental divide, it was near the end of March. Here, while the eastern slope from the watershed was very long and gradual to the heads of the eastern rivers, the west side was very much steeper and shorter in distance to the heads of the rivers. In fact, one could walk from the watershed to where we later built our boats in a day . . .
>
> I think about seventy-five people came through this route. A few were ahead of us, but many far behind, and, of course, many got fed up with the hard work and extreme cold and went back . . .
>
> Well, we came down the western slope until we reached a place where sufficient timber grew to a size out of which we could whipsaw lumber to build another boat for the final stage of our long trip. Here again many new partnerships were formed. My partner and I joined up with a young doctor and his father whom we had met, and liked, on the trail. We whipsawed lumber and built a boat, and as soon as the ice went out were ready to start. Now, when the ice broke up and moved out, what had appeared to be a good-sized river showed up for what it was, just a swift, shallow, rocky stream. But we now had to take things as they were, so we loaded up and cast off into a swift, swirling mass of water and foam. We had gone perhaps half a mile when the boat was lifted up and crashed on a rock, making a hole in the bottom. We pulled ashore, unloaded and turned the boat up and patched and recaulked it. Next day we were ready to make another start. We now had better luck, and emerged into a much larger stream, which, while good for short distances, had rapids and canyons on and off for two hundred miles. This was a daily hazard to parties drifting down an unknown river, but we were lucky, and came through without mishap, while several others suffered damage to their boats and goods.

In a couple of terse sentences, Corp sums up hundreds of miles of river travel, river travel that we, experienced whitewater paddlers with modern equipment, found challenging. Maybe he'd survived so many hardships by then that things like rapids were of little consequence. Maybe all his nerves had been frostbitten in the struggle over the continental divide. But maybe, he just wanted to forget. One of the mysteries in Corp's narrative concerns the death of Victor McFarland.

June is the high-water month for the rivers that drain the western slopes of the Selwyn Mountains. On June 6, 1899, the water was brown and turbulent. Logs, plucked from sand bars by the rising river, jostled the boats. Victor McFarland clutched the rough wooden sides of his boat . . . until the sweep, the long wooden oar used for steering, swept him into the river.

It was tough just keeping these boats afloat, much less maneuvering for rescue. McFarland's companions found his body a kilometer downstream. They hacked out a shallow grave, lined it with spruce boughs, and paid their last respects. Then they got back in their boat, and shoved off.

Corp doesn't write about any deaths on this portion of the journey, only damage to "boats and goods." This is especially odd, since Victor McFarland was from Hamilton, and part of Corp's original party.

August 1987

In the shadow of Keele Peak, the river bed of the Hess is strewn with water-polished boulders. It's as though someone has gathered up the rapids in the Rock Gardens on the South Nahanni and squeezed them into a couple of pulse-pounding kilometers. We while away two days picking our way through the rapids, scouting every inch. We run several rapids that we should have portaged, and portage one rapid that we wanted to run. Our only casualty is one paddle, torn from the velcro straps on Rachel and Graham's spray cover by a wave that swept across the deck.

Below Keele Creek the rapids are no longer continuous, and we have time to look around. Bold ridges on the north side of the river climb into the granite summits of the Rogue Range. We stop and hike for several days, once again dragging our climbing gear hundreds of vertical meters above the river, once again retreating when clouds and showers obscure the mountains.

We paddle on and encounter a large tributary that drains the southern flanks of the Keele Peak massif. This, I think, is the stream by which Ernest Corp and company descended to the Hess.

Unlike the MacMillan, to the south, or the Stewart, to the north, the rapids on the Hess don't end as the river leaves the Selwyn Mountains. It seems as though the whitewater rolls upriver to meet us, in sets, like Pacific swells crashing on a rocky headland.

We travel for several days, floating through a natural art gallery. Stone statues, sculpted by wind and water, stand in the river. Molded canyons force the river inwards, and we enter watchfully. Mountain ranges appear to rise upward at our approach. They dominate the landscape, then recede into the background.

Three wolves watch us from behind the trees. The adult vanishes in the shadows, but the pups lope along the bank, keeping abreast. We float past the mouth of the Rogue River and the wolves stop. They stand, forelegs straight, and watch as we drift out of sight.

"I need a hit of chocolate," says Rachel.

We're drifting together. Alpine peaks have given way to low wooded hills and there haven't been any big rapids all day. Wendy digs in the food bag. "There's only one bar left," she says.

"It's calling to us," says Rachel. "It wants to be eaten."

We float around a corner and I hear a deep throbbing. I sit up. The Hess is a full-grown river now, swollen by the inflow of tributaries. The current strengthens. I can see a horizon line and the sharp, clean lines of rock walls. I swallow my last square of chocolate and grab my paddle.

We drag our canoes onto a sandy beach and scramble over logs jammed against the exposed bedrock. They've been carelessly tossed here, like huge pick-up-sticks, by the powerful flows of high water.

The last rapid on the Hess.

"What do you think?" Rachel asks.

"I think we should run it in two stages," I answer slowly. "We'll have to back ferry to the center of the river to miss those holes, and cut across the standing waves into the eddy. We can worry about the rest of the rapid later."

"Just a minute," says Wendy, her forehead furrowed. "When do we start paddling forward?"

"Okay," I say. "See the edge of the hole? When we pass that, we should be moving forward, pointing right."

Graham sets up his tripod and fiddles with his camera. I hand the other camera to Rachel. The throw lines are on the rocks next to their feet. Wendy and I walk back, turning to look at the rapid from different angles, making sure that we know where the current lines are heading, making sure that we'll recognize the hole from river level.

I kneel in the bow, pull up the spray skirt, and look back. "You ready?" She nods. We ferry out and turn downstream.

"Back ferry left," I say. I dig my blade into the water and sweep it towards the bow, putting my back into it. The heavy canoe slowly edges towards the middle. We're far enough over to clear the hole, but I want to make sure we have momentum towards shore when we reach it.

"Okay, forward!" I yell. We slash through a large standing wave, its crest breaking over the canoe and slapping me in the chest. I brace, draw the bow to the right, and paddle hard. The canoe slams into the eddy and turns with the grace of a water buffalo in maple syrup. At least we're upright. I take a deep breath.

Wendy ties the canoe to a jammed log. I put down my paddle and climb up on the rock shelf. I squint through the view finder of the camera and twirl the focusing ring. Graham and Rachel step into their canoe.

I snap a couple of photos as Rachel and Graham backpaddle to line up. They squirt past the edge of the hole at the same spot we did, but with their bow angled away from shore. Sensing doom, I forget the camera and look up. They pivot to head for the eddy, but a curling wave engulfs their stern.

"Oh-oh," says Wendy, "they're over."

I grab the throwline, but they're already out of reach — and anyway, the size and strength of the river would have made a rope more of an emotional sop than a practical tool. A wave buries Rachel, and she bobs up downstream. They wash out of sight around the corner of a rock wall.

I run to the end of the canyon with the throw rope. Two saturated bodies are splashing in the shallows several hundred meters downstream, towing the protesting canoe.

"They're okay," I yell to Wendy.

"I'm bringing the first aid kit anyway," she says.

"Bring some dry clothes too."

In the hot sunshine, it's more amusing than it might have been. The only casualties are their two paddles, somewhere downstream, making a break for freedom. Graham and Rachel spread their soggy clothing on the rocks.

"It's lucky we ate the chocolate," says Rachel.

Wendy and I walk back to run the bottom half of the rapid. "We only have three paddles left," says Wendy. "Hold on to your paddle if we flip."

We come close to dumping, but we survive the final breaking wave. As soon as the gear is dry, we paddle downstream. With one paddle, Graham and Rachel limp along near shore. We stay on the other side hoping to see a black handle protruding from a tangle of driftwood, or floating in an eddy.

Summer 1899

We still didn't know what river we were on, but thought maybe it was the Pelly River, until one day we saw a large blaze on a tree, on which was written, "This is the South Fork of the Stewart River, fifty miles above the Fraser Falls." We had heard of the Fraser Falls, and thought, "here is another dangerous hazard to navigate," but were pleased to find it could be easily side passed by hauling boats and goods across a flat shoulder of rocks, on skids, a very short distance. Then the boats were dropped back into the water and reloaded immediately below the falls.

From here on it was a pleasure trip after what we had come through, as even a steamboat from Dawson can come up the river.

We arrived at the mouth of the Mayo River, where now is the town of Mayo. At that time there were just a few shacks and a trading post and the Indian village just below across the river.

August 1987

The run-away paddles remain hidden, although we continue the search until we reach the Stewart River. The next morning we lash the canoes together. At first, three of us paddle while the fourth reads or dozes. Then, to balance our thrust, just the stern paddlers work.

It's my turn in the bow and I look up from my book at the sound of a quavering shriek. There is a circle of ripples ahead, and the wail still hangs in the air. A red-throated loon surfaces, neck stretched, webbed feet windmilling. Its low-slung body arrows downriver and it lifts off gradually, like a float plane, circling to gain elevation.

The story of a river sojourn cannot be completely told in words and I wonder about the things unsaid by Ernest J. Corp. He doesn't write about the land, except as an adversary to be beaten back. He doesn't describe wolves, or caribou, or loons. He uses no adjectives to describe beauty.

I can't believe that our perceptions have changed so radically in less than a century.

We carry our canoes past Fraser Falls and paddle in a dwindling current towards Mayo. We deal with the usual regrets at the end of a trip. Water and sky bartered for dust and exhaust.

I do look forward to a cold beer though. And a hot shower.

Dawson City during the gold rush. Photo courtesy Public Archives of Canada.

FIRTH RIVER

OF CARIBOU AND OIL

Part I: The Arctic National Wildlife Refuge

The Gwich'in are caribou people, the northernmost Indian tribe in North America. Their ancestral lands sprawl across the northern edge of the international boundary between Alaska and the Yukon.

The migratory wanderings of the Porcupine caribou herd are through Gwich'in lands, on both sides of the border. The path of the caribou is dictated by the physical features of the land, not by political boundaries.

The caribou are the basis of Gwich'in culture and life.

In the summer, the great herds are restless, milling throngs. Nearly 200,000 caribou of the Porcupine herd congregate on the coastal plains to the north of Alaska's Brooks Range. Cows with young calves assemble in knots and wander eastward. Soon the bulls join them, the individual caribou behaving like the cells of a larger organism.

The herd usually crosses the Firth River sometime in July, their migratory route swinging south through the British Mountains. They scatter towards wintering grounds as the greens of summer fade. Some turn east, wandering through the Richardson Mountains and towards the Mackenzie Delta. Many traverse the Old Crow Flats and winter in the high country across the Alaska border. Others wander south, to the Bell River and Rat Pass country.

In the spring, the pregnant cows return to the land of their own birth, to the north slope in Alaska, to the Arctic National Wildlife Refuge (ANWR). There they drift apart and drop their calves. The herd's cycle of life is renewed.

The calving ground on the coastal plain is a pivotal point in the controversy surrounding oil exploration and development in ANWR.

In 1960, U.S. President Dwight Eisenhower announced that 3.6 million hectares in Alaska, including the Arctic coastal plain near the Canadian border, would be set aside "for the purpose of preserving unique wildlife, wilderness, and recreational values . . ." Canada was slow to follow, but in 1978, it too withdrew a large tract of land, more than 3.7 million hectares.

The Porcupine caribou herd symbolizes the wilderness wealth in these lands, but many other animals live here, including polar bears, grizzlies, wolves, wolverines, moose, and musk oxen. The refuge is a critical staging area for snow geese. Peregrine falcons, Arctic gyrfalcons, golden eagles, swans, and myriad shore birds nest in the mountains and in the coastal plain.

The internal combustion engine has bestowed an unprecedented freedom of movement in the western world. The automobile is king. To commuters in metal shells, the Arctic is a frozen wasteland, a place for explorers to conquer, then leave. Leave to the howling blizzards and the lemmings.

During the 1970s, the OPEC oil cartel pushed the price of petroleum to record heights. "They're holding us ransom!" shouted North Americans, asserting their right to drive luxury cars wherever and whenever they chose. "We must become self-sufficient in oil production."

In Prudhoe Bay, Alaska, millions of barrels of oil already flowed freely through the Trans-Alaska Pipeline towards Valdez. Unfortunately for the Gwich'in, unfortunately for the caribou and the snow geese, oil companies turned their attention eastward, where seeps of crude oil indicated that reservoirs of hydrocarbons might also lie beneath the surface of the coastal plain of ANWR.

Oil and gas carried more weight with legislators than did wildlife and indigenous peoples. In 1980, the Alaska National Interest Lands Conservation Act created a legacy of parks and wildlife refuges. The Arctic coastal plain was excluded, until the environmental impacts of petroleum exploration and development could be assessed, and until seismic studies could estimate the oil reserves.

The draft study, released in 1986, outlined potentially devastating effects on wildlife if exploration and development went ahead. Grizzly and wolverine populations could be reduced by half or more. The birds — the snow geese, the swans, the shore birds, and the raptors — could be displaced from breeding and staging areas. And the Porcupine caribou herd, symbol of the strength and fragility of the Arctic, could suffer a population decline and change in distribution of up to 72,000 animals.

All for oil.

The studies that outlined the environmental impacts of exploration and drilling also looked at the richness of the oil fields. According to the U.S. Department of the Interior, there is only a nineteen percent chance that any recoverable oil will be found. And, if recoverable oil is discovered, the median estimate is only about three billion barrels . . . a two-hundred-day supply for the United States.

Heightened energy efficiency in automobiles could save 400,000 barrels of oil per day, far more than ANWR could produce. Instead, during the Reagan years, speed limits on highways were raised and energy-saving programs cut. In 1988, Transportation Secretary James Burnley called for the repeal of automobile efficiency standards because " . . . fuel economy rules are handicapping our companies in facing the new competition from foreign manufacturers in larger, more luxurious models."

If exploratory drilling is given the green light, the face of the Porcupine herd's calving ground will be forever changed. A small industrial city will spring up in the heart of the refuge. Airfields, ports, desalinization plants, and production facilities will be constructed. Hundreds of kilometers of roads and pipelines will crisscross the land. The exploration will take place at up to one hundred drilling pads. Each pad will blanket several hectares of tundra, and suck up to 60,000,000 liters of water from this arctic desert.

Gravel is scarce, and would be mined in enormous quantities. At Prudhoe Bay, almost five thousand hectares have been covered by gravel, and tens of thousands more are blighted with dust or contaminated with chemicals. Since 1972, there have been an estimated seventeen thousand oil spills on Alaska's north slope.

In March of 1990, Wendy Boothroyd and I drive over the coastal mountain pass to Haines, Alaska, where I am scheduled to give a slide show about the mining threat to the Tatshenshini River. In the interior, the land is still white, with patches of brown on south-facing slopes. On the coast, the sudden brightness of new growth and rich smells of spring are a shock.

We go to a meeting of the Lynn Canal Conservation group after the slide show. We stretch out on the floor. Someone passes me a mug of herbal tea and a plate of chocolate chip cookies. I sip the tea, listening to talk about a mine near Juneau, about ore truck traffic through Haines, about clearcut logging in the Tongass National Forest. A tortoiseshell cat walks across the living room floor and rubs against my legs. It lifts its head against my hand and I scratch its backbone.

"There's one good thing about the Valdez oil spill," says a man sprawled in the pool of light from a standing lamp. "They'll never dare open ANWR to oil development now."

But now there is increased turmoil in the Middle East. Oil wells burn and the world's largest oil slick drifts menacingly through the Persian Gulf. In Los Angeles, in Vancouver, in Chicago, lines of automobiles rush into city centers and back to the suburbs. Back and forth. More cars every day.

And voices that insist on oil development in ANWR are again raised in the Alaska legislature and in the U.S. Congress.

The Gwich'in are not a part of the war effort. They have no control over North America's insatiable appetite for oil. They only wish to maintain their way of life, a way of life that has sustained them for centuries.

Part II: The Firth River

January 1991

It isn't so much the cold: you get used to minus thirty-degree temperatures. It's the wind, the wind that speeds down from the north, whirling the dry snow into devils that dance through downtown Whitehorse towards the Yukon River. The wind finds chinks in my clothes no matter how often I zip up my jacket and tighten my scarf.

It's hot inside the hotel. I shove my jacket, mitts, toque, and scarf into my day pack, but I'm afraid that I might be late, so I don't walk into the bathroom to strip off my long underwear. I look around the lobby, which is a zoo of stuffed animals.

A zoo of stuffed animals.

Behind the reception desk are the predators. A black wolf's lips are curled back in a permanent snarl. A lynx leers at me with a macabre laugh, eyes slitted and ears pointed back. The arctic fox has a benign expression. I walk past the head of a moose, a Dall sheep, a stone sheep. A mangy ptarmigan is frozen in flight, wings outstretched against a rounded wooden burl. There is even a moth-eaten African impala. The caribou antlers have no head. Just the antlers, glued to a plaque.

Norma Kassi is already waiting at a small table cluttered with cups, saucers, and silverware. Behind her is a print of a tall ship battered by stormy seas. Her parka is on the back of her chair. "It's so cold," she says, pulling it over her shoulders.

"You must be used to it," I answer, "this must be normal for someone from Old Crow."

"No, at home we dress for it. Here, I'm in and out of buildings . . . out from the warmth, into the cold."

The waitress is standing beside me with a glass carafe of coffee. I turn over my cup. This isn't the restaurant that I would have chosen, but it is quiet on a Friday afternoon. There are only a few people scattered at tables, stretching out their coffee refills, postponing the extreme wind chills.

"I'm a bit nervous," I say. "I've been interviewed about environmental issues a number of times, but this is the first time I've interviewed someone else."

She smiles. She is wearing a white blouse with splotches of bright colour. A pendant dangles from her neck, a simple ring of metal encircling the silhouette of a bull caribou. It's what we've come to talk about. I ask her what the Porcupine caribou herd means to her, to her people.

"I can't imagine what it would be like not to have the caribou," she says. "It's a vital animal to us. It's the connection between us and the land." She looks away as she describes her homeland, up and over my shoulder at the prints on the wall, but her dark brown eyes aren't focused there. Her body is across the table, but for the moment she's far away.

"Our whole life line, our laws, our values, our spiritual life . . . they all revolve around the caribou." She speaks of the past, beginning sentences with "we," even though she's talking of a time before her birth. The blending of the past, present, and future is real to her in a way that I can accept intellectually, but that is alien to me emotionally.

White people have been drawn to the Arctic for centuries. Successful explorers, like Vilhjalmur Stefansson, studied the native peoples and learned to live with the rhythms of the land. Less perceptive ones, like Captain John Franklin, tried to impose their own rigid patterns, to bludgeon the Arctic into submission.

Franklin was the first European to see the Firth River. In 1825, he set sail from Liverpool, England, with his trusted aides Lieutenant Back and Dr. Richardson. They had had the dubious privilege of accompanying Franklin on his journey to the the polar sea during 1819-1822. Starvation, murder, and cannibalism had highlighted that trip. They must have had hearts of oak to subject themselves to Franklin's orders again.

After overwintering on Great Bear Lake, the party floated down the Mackenzie to the Arctic Ocean. Franklin sailed west, battling pack ice and storms, ". . . tormented the whole way by myriads of musquitoes."

As the party navigated through the shallows between Herschel Island and the mainland, they met a group of Inuit with iron, knives, and beads. Franklin became hopeful — since these people must be trading with the Russians, surely the Pacific couldn't be *that* far. He discovered that the goods had come from Inuit who lived far to the west and "also from the Indians, who came every year from the Interior to trade with them by a river . . . which I have, therefore, named the Mountain Indian River."

Franklin's discoveries fueled his drive to seek the Northwest Passage, a quest that was to claim his life and the lives of his entire crew in 1847. The Mountain Indian River was later renamed for John Firth, Hudson's Bay Company Factor at Ramparts House on the Porcupine River.

The wave of white people who followed the explorers were interested in translating the natural wealth of the north into personal wealth. Fur traders, musk ox hunters, whalers, gold miners, and most recently, searchers for oil.

Ben Moise, Graham Wilson, Wendy Boothroyd, and I aren't immune from the spell of the Arctic. We make plans to drive to Inuvik in early July and fly to Margaret Lake, close to the Alaska-Yukon border and a few hundred meters from the Firth River. We'll fly out from Herschel Island two weeks later.

July 1989

Cr-r-ruck! Prruk! I burrow into my sleeping bag, wishing the ravens would choose somewhere else to deliver their wake-up calls. *Prruk! Tok!* I lift my head groggily. Four a.m. sunshine pierces the tent walls, bathing Wendy's face in an unearthly blue glow and super-heating the stale air. Corpses of mosquitoes, encased in dried smears of our own blood, dangle from the insect netting. My ears still buzz from our marathon, 1250-kilometer drive up the Klondike and Dempster highways in Graham's VW van.

We stagger out of sleeping bags, sort our gear at the float plane dock, and drive into Inuvik to find the office of the recently created Northern Yukon National Park. I had called park officials from Whitehorse, but we need to finish our bureaucratic hoop-jumping by picking up a permit to float the Firth River.

We dutifully complete our paperwork, and find an open cafeteria. A blue haze of cigarette smoke warns of the futility of looking for a non-smoking section. Ben, rediscovering his northern Ontario roots, feels instantly at home. Wearing his baseball cap as a badge of respectability, he slips behind a chipped arborite table and begins talking with the locals. Graham, Wendy, and I, confirmed vegetarians, stare dubiously at the menu posted above the grill. The coffee looks and tastes like motor oil. It doesn't make me feel any better, but it opens my eyes for the drive back to the lake.

Tangles of bright yellow polypropylene cord litter the hard-packed dirt in front of the dock. A young man in jeans and a black western shirt wrestles with Ben's kayak on the pontoon of a Cessna 185, lassoing it with coil after coil of rope.

The pilot, an older fellow wearing shiny green polyester pants, slouches nearby. The material of his matching shirt strains over his beer belly, showing patches of a dirty white T-shirt in the gaps between the buttons. Sweat beads on his forehead. He lights a cigarette from the butt of another and wheezes, "Gimme more rope!" Apparently more layers are required to mummify the kayak.

Most pilots are quick and efficient with external loads, touchy if ham-fisted customers stray too near — but these two look helpless with ropes. "Would you like some help?" I ask diffidently.

"You tied knots before?"

I nod, and soon Wendy and I are standing on the pontoon, using the tricks learned in decades of securing boats onto roof racks. We tie trucker's hitches to cinch the kayaks to the struts and lash down the grab loops. The fat pilot and his lackey retire to the cool interior of the office.

"Wendy, do you think that pilot will make it to the Firth without having a heart attack?" I ask.

A harsh yell rolls from an open window and cuts off her reply, "Any you guys got a map?"

Ben walks into the office with a map while Wendy discusses tactics with Graham. "Attempting CPR in midflight would be tricky. You'd be better off shoving him out of the way and trying to land the plane yourself."

It turns out that two planes, flying in tandem, will take us to the Firth. We draw straws to see who will fly with the second pilot. Wendy and I win.

Our pilot is a young man with a paunch and a sour expression. He introduces himself with a harangue about his employer. "Don't be surprised if someone else flies you out from Herschel Island. I'm quitting after this flight. This outfit is so goddam cheap. My pay checks are always late, and always short. The last one was $218 light. So bloody cheap."

Wendy climbs into the rear of the plane and squats on a life jacket that has been placed in lieu of a seat. We look at the ratty upholstery. In the middle of the instrument panel there is a rectangular hole with protruding wires. Outside, pockmarks adorn the wings and fuselage.

"Hey, don't get me wrong!" says our pilot. "The aircraft are fine... they're just so goddam cheap."

Our plane takes off a few minutes after Ben and Graham's. We gain altitude and the expansive maze of channels, lakes, and islands in the Mackenzie Delta open up below us. As we drone towards the mountainous country to the west, the radiophone crackles. "I'm on your tail, Big Boy." I look back. The fat pilot had circled until we were airborne, to follow us and avoid the task of route finding.

In the other plane, Ben decides to snap some pictures of the delta. He holds his camera close to the window and leans against the door. As he adjusts the exposure, the door flies open.

"Sorry about that," says the pilot nervously, reaching across to grab the handle. A sign on the window in bold letters reads, "Only the Pilot to secure this door."

Our joy at landing on Margaret Lake is part happiness to reach the wilderness, part relief at surviving our flights.

January 1991

"What was it like to grow up in Old Crow?" I ask.

"Our life in the northern Yukon revolves around the caribou," she says. "They come to visit in the fall and again in the spring. They come faithfully. Our people are low-spirited in the times before they come, but after, spirits are high. It's a renewal of life."

The waitress is again hovering with the coffee. "Just half a cup," I say. Norma shakes her head. I add cream and stir in a spoonful of sugar.

"I started helping with the caribou as soon as I could walk. But my connection with them started even before that." She picks up her empty cup, looks into it, and puts it back down. "I was allergic to cow's milk, and my mother couldn't breast feed me. I was given juice from caribou meat right from birth."

"I haven't been to Old Crow," I say, "but we could see the Old Crow Flats when we flew into the headwaters of the Firth."

"Our people used to build caribou fences near the Firth," she says, "wooden fences to herd the caribou so they could hunt them."

She sits up and looks at me. "And my grandfathers used to go across the Old Crow Flats, over the mountains, and down the Firth to trade at Herschel Island. They always brought back goodies."

She is smiling as though she has just popped one of those goodies into her mouth. For the moment, she looks so pleased I can almost taste it with her. "They never made that trip," she says, "after I was born."

July 1989

It is hot and the sun won't set. Still shaky from the driving and the flight, we sprawl in our tents and doze. None of us have watches, and the only way we can guess the time is to take a compass bearing from the sun that is angling above the horizon. Sometime the next day, we ferry across the Firth to hike into the mountains.

Hummocks sprout above the permafrost less than a meter below. I settle into a jerky gait, like a marionette, squelching through soggy pools of moss. Upland sandpipers fly into the wind, their curved wings catching updrafts that allow them to hover briefly before settling on flimsy willow perches. A stockier bird arrows past. I expect to identify an unfamiliar northern species. I don't know why I'm surprised to find robins this far north.

The blossoms in the valley are past their prime. At higher elevations though, arctic poppies, alpine forget-me-nots, and paintbrushes brighten the complexion of the hillsides. I flop down to catch my breath beside a white flower with a delicate rose blush.

Fossilized seashells.

Wendy leafs through a field guide. "I think it's an elegant paintbrush," she says. "It says here that they only grow north of the sixty-seventh parallel."

We climb a ridge that terminates in eroding hoodoos, eerie pillars that stand like sentinels. I step on an unusual rock, stoop, and examine it — a large fossil. Now that I've discovered one, dozens jump out as we toil upward. Imprinted in the limestone are pieces of coral and spiral shells. I look at the mountains, trying to imagine the land submerged under the sea.

The peaks are interconnected by chestnut and ochre ridges. The land looks familiar, yet oddly different. The valleys are V-shaped, weathered by millions of years of wind and precipitation rather than scoured by glaciers. Despite its harsh climate, the northern Yukon escaped the Quaternary glaciation which flooded most of Canada with ice.

The ridge sweeps in an arc back towards the Firth, which foams north and vanishes behind a mountain shoulder. I've backpacked with too many joint-crunching loads, and my knees tremble with loathing when we begin to descend. We zigzag down a broad slope to a gravelly creek that empties into the river near our camp.

Near the mouth of the creek, we stumble upon a pit, a rectangular cavity with ragged edges. An arctic poppy stirs in the gentle breeze, pushing up through broken glass, cans, and rusting shovels.

We find another dump in the meadow beside Margaret Lake.

The next day we load our kayaks and slide into the river. The Firth propels us swiftly downstream.

Ben had talked with biologists, botanists, and historians before our trip, noting points of interest on his maps. The words "caribou fence" are written with an arrow pointing to contour lines just east of the Firth, not far below Margaret Lake. We find a gravel bar below the hill and set up camp.

I brush away bugs as I prepare supper. The others hide in the tents. Mosquitoes cling to the netting, like visitors to a zoo. The air is hot, humid, and windless, but I put on pants and a long-sleeved shirt. I wish that I had had the sense to bring a head net and bug jacket. I move as I cook, stirring with one hand and flicking the other around my head and neck.

"It's ready," I call, even though the pasta is still crunchy. We eat on the run.

"Let's get moving," says Wendy.

The insects, annoying at camp, become insufferable as we walk across the gravel bar into the trees. Our evening stroll escalates into a jog, then a sprint. I drape a raincoat over my head. Clouds form under my improvised shelter and a salty rain begins to drip.

Wendy and friends.

Biologists, when they aren't banding or radio-collaring anything that moves, spend much of their work week lost in speculation. How *do* insects affect the psyche of caribou? Why *do* they flee to hill crests, searching for wind? What *is* all that frenzied running and snorting about? There must be a PhD thesis in this somewhere.

I am at one with caribou at that moment, dashing uphill, hoping that a breeze is stirring the willows on the crest. It isn't.

We don't find the caribou fence, but then again, we don't linger to search thoroughly.

Another broiling afternoon, horseflies drone and a family of northern shrikes performs an open-air concert. Their harsh, jay-like shrieks are jazzed by melodious warbling interludes. They flutter off in a black and white flurry of feathers.

Joe Creek, a large, braided tributary, is fed by sheets of overflow ice that last through the summer. A finger of gravel juts out where the two streams meet, forming a deep eddy. Wendy and I strip in the sunshine, revealing our Yukon kayaker's tan. Our hands and faces are ruddy brown, the rest of our bodies mushroom-coloured. A bath had seemed reasonable a couple of hours earlier, inside a steamy dry suit, but now I stare at the water doubtfully. Wendy plunges in, splashing a wave of water that laps at my toes. I stand ankle deep, dabbling half-heartedly. She has a self-satisfied glow as we walk to our tent.

In the evening we ferry across the river. A few mosquitoes pursue us through the narrow belt of spruce growing near the water. After the hordes of the previous evening, we laugh at them. We can appreciate the country instead of concentrating on survival.

A wail pierces the hush. A peregrine falcon labours into the sky with staccato wing beats, looking ponderous, clumsy. The shredded remains of a songbird droop in the boughs of a spruce. A beak hangs suspended in a bloody mass of flesh. Feathers litter the ground. Stark evidence that a peregrine is anything but clumsy during its plunging pursuit of prey.

We hike out of the trees and onto a ridge. Fertile growth carpets the valley, an olive strip that merges with broad meadows and emerald knolls. Green. Everything is green, except the limestone summits. Shadows sweep across the landscape, turning it into a verdant kaleidoscope.

"Hey Wendy," I say, "if we had been whisked away from Whitehorse and mystically transported here, where would you guess we are?"

"The Scottish moors," says Wendy.

"Maybe the foothills of the Karakoram?" I suggest.

"It's pretty arid to the north," says Wendy, "it looks like the Canyonlands in Utah."

I would never guess 69 degrees latitude, on the Yukon's North Slope.

We had heard that the Firth had difficult rapids, and before long the river vanishes into the yawning mouth of a gorge. We climb out of our kayaks to scout from shore.

River runners use more than the sense of sight while scouting. I scramble across exposed bedrock, my hands gripping smooth, water-polished stone. The rumbling sounds of the rapids change in pitch and swell in volume at our approach.

A falsetto whine, no longer the voice of the Firth, overpowers the growling of whitewater. A helicopter speeds past, banks, and zooms overhead. A faceless person leans over, clicking the shutter release of a camera. The whirring drowns other sensations and we stare, mesmerized like moose in the glare of headlights. At length the helicopter drones northward.

The presence of the river returns slowly.

Thunder mutters and echoes off the cliffs, a cue that our un-Arctic-like weather is ending. We paddle through the first series of bouncy rapids in the Firth's forty-kilometer-long canyon. Ben flips in a hole behind a ledge and immediately rolls up. Not far downstream, we beach our kayaks at the confluence of Sheep Creek, on a sandy beach concealed in a niche in the rock walls.

Up the creek, a helicopter lifts off. A maple leaf flag stirs in the blast of air. Fourteen buildings squat on the bank, not counting the outhouses. It's the headquarters of Northern Yukon National Park.

Flipping in a hole.

Arctic poppy.

    A chaos of mine tailings parallels the creek, the legacy of a placer gold mine of the 1950s. A bulldozer rusts on a gravel bar, flanked by listing oil drums, a derelict backhoe, and the rusting coils of a bedspring. We cache our gear in our tents and trudge through the tailings.

    Wendy and I walk into a large A-frame, looking for the warden. Boxes of food and gear are piled against the wall. There are a few books on a plank. Two people stand beside a wooden table staring at a map. They glance at us, but say nothing.

    Wendy picks up a field guide to birds, "Look," she says, "it *was* a golden plover."

    The warden looks over, as though annoyed at our intrusion. He is tall and thin with neatly brushed hair. He wears the official light green uniform complete with epaulettes. Next to him stands a stocky man with tinted glasses and an artistically arranged scarf, jabbing his fingers towards the map. "This ridge is twelve minutes away," he says.

I walk over and look at the contour lines. They are pointing to a mountain that we had climbed two days upriver. Twelve minutes?

"Do you want to film a wolf den?" asks the warden.

"Time! We need more time! We have to be in Herschel the day after tomorrow," says the man, rolling up the maps and putting them under his arm. He nods to me and walks out.

"Helicopter schedules!" says the warden, shaking my hand. "They want to get their filming done. We need to get supplies to finish construction of these buildings."

"Who's filming?" I ask.

"It's a crew getting footage for CBC's "The Nature of Things" and for *National Geographic*."

We walk outside. A fat ground squirrel balances on its hind legs and chatters a shrill demand for food. A young woman wearing an apron sits on wooden steps leading from the door of an old house trailer. She shreds a piece of bread and tosses chunks down to the squirrel. "Come by for supper," she says to Wendy and I. "We eat in two shifts. Maybe in about two hours?"

A man walks by, wearing a tool belt and carrying a board. Behind an outhouse, a pair of Dall sheep, a ewe and a lamb, graze languidly. They've been lured from the mountains by a mineral lick originally set out by miners.

We come back later for supper. In the center of the cook shack trailer are several long, metal tables. Bowls and platters are lined up along the counter against the wall — salads, meat dishes, and six varieties of dessert. "The crab legs are on the stove," says the cook, "help yourself."

Thunder growls outside, and slanting lines of rain splatter against the metal sides of the trailer. Inside it is warm, and the film crew are telling us about their experiences.

"The caribou herd is still in Alaska," says the man with the scarf. "The helicopter put us down with them a few days ago. Magical."

I drink another cup of coffee and watch the rain through the window.

Wendy and I walk outside and cross the creek. I didn't come to the Arctic to look at the inside of walls, but creature comforts attract me more than I like to admit. We crawl into our tent. Ben and Graham have decided to borrow bunks inside a high-tech, semipermanent wall tent.

Late in the morning, I wake to rain still pattering on the tent fly. I open a book and read for about an hour. The rain stops. The helicopter warms up about fifty meters from Ben and Graham's shelter. It lifts off and flies over our heads towards the south. It returns half an hour later, touches down briefly and clatters off again, this time towards Herschel Island.

"Even those two couldn't sleep through that," says Wendy as we spread the tent on the rocks to dry.

Later, I track down the warden and tell him about the trash we'd found upriver.

"It's a problem," he admits, "but some bureaucrats say that the stuff miners left behind has human heritage value."

"What about the bulldozers and garbage along the creek here?"

He shrugs. "That too."

I wonder if it would be okay for us to leave our tin-foil wrappers and plastic bags. They must have human heritage value, too.

"Why are you building a permanent outpost here?" I ask.

He launches into a series of justifications. Stopping poaching. Interpreting natural history for visitors. Safety. "River runners are happy enough to have us here when they get into trouble." He sounds a little petulant, as though he has answered that question before.

Wendy and I hike into the mountains. From a ridge, I see a pair of sheep, maybe the same ones I'd seen yesterday. They are silhouetted against a swath of placer tailings snaking up Sheep Creek.

We return in midafternoon and walk over to Ben and Graham's hutch. I unzip the door and poke my head inside. It is a steam bath that smells like polypropylene long underwear after a week inside a dry suit.

"Graham? Ben?" A lump inside the dim interior rolls over.

"Ben?"

"What?"

"How could you sleep through the noise of the helicopter?"

"What helicopter?"

"We're ready to go any time," I say.

Half a dozen people from the compound gather at the river to watch us leave. The first person to paddle the Firth had been a solo kayaker, but since then, only rafts have floated down the river.

"Where do you fit all your gear?" asks a young Inuit from the Mackenzie Delta who is training to be a warden. He squats beside my kayak and sticks his head into the cockpit.

"We have to travel lighter than rafters," I say.

Everyone likes to watch Eskimo rolls. Even an Inuit. I flip, roll up, and wave goodbye. Folds of bedrock flash under us as we paddle downstream.

"Ki-ki-ki!" I look up at a merlin perched on a promontory, scolding us. Higher, against a backdrop of lofty cumulus, a golden eagle soars, its dark silhouette gilded by bronze flashes. It uses the surges of wind as we do river currents.

We paddle for an hour, then camp. I hike upward through rocky tors and crags, relieved to be away from the camp, relieved to be back in the wilderness.

A young female caribou appears in front of me, her chest floating in front of powerful legs, her head held high. She stops to gape back every few seconds, unsure if I am an enemy. The slopes above are scored with a maze of trails from migrations of the Porcupine herd. The land seems still, holding its breath, waiting for the herd.

January 1991

"I was elected as Old Crow MLA in 1985," Norma says. "Or was it 1986? I can't remember, but that's when I started lobbying against oil development in the Arctic National Wildlife Refuge."

"It seems that the issue will be decided in large southern cities," I say. "But you have to live with the impact in Old Crow."

"It's overwhelming," she says. "People in those areas live for today, not for the future. Not for our grandchildren."

She is silent for a moment. "I've gone to California several times, to Washington D.C., to Honolulu, to Denver. I'm going to Memphis and Oregon soon. When I started lobbying, I met so many young white people who were just like me. Except they were searching. Searching for some connection with the land. They'd listen and they'd look at the slides of Old Crow Flats that I brought. Then they'd begin to see."

"Sometimes I'm very discouraged when I go back to Old Crow after I've been away. The elders sit me down, and they make me think. Some of the elders have never been out of Old Crow, but still they see the spiritual connections."

"Our elders, for a while, had to deal with people who broke the old laws. Some young people would get trigger-happy and kill too many caribou, more than we could use. Our elders would say that if we broke the old laws, one day there would be no caribou left for our people."

Firth canyon.

July 1989

"Watch the canyon," they had said back in Whitehorse, "especially after it rains. The rapids are big. And they're continuous."

It rains while we are in the canyon, but the river doesn't rise. The rapids aren't big, and they aren't continuous. We are all disappointed that the whitewater isn't more challenging. I sling a camera around my neck and clamber up a gully for a falcon's eye view of the last rapids.

Wendy and Graham ride the standing waves in the main downstream tongue, but Ben casually floats into the foaming mouth of a diagonal hole. His red kayak disappears. The hole swallows him, chews his boat for a moment, and spits him out, upside-down. From my eyrie I can see swift green water bubbling over boulders and the crimson bottom of Ben's kayak.

Swimming on the Firth.

A white paddle blade rises to the surface and probes the bubbling froth like the searching tentacle of a giant squid. The kayak pirouettes as it wallows to right itself. A helmeted head emerges, gasps for oxygen, and submerges.

The paddle again surfaces, this time for a textbook roll. Tuck. Paddle sweep. Hip flick. Remember to keep your head down . . . but, as Ben comes up, he washes into another hole. I see nothing of him for several heartbeats. He sets up for a final attempt, but his boat slams into a boulder. The swift current flattens him between kayak and stone. Slowly, grudgingly, the boat cartwheels downriver.

Ben is out of air. He pulls off his spray deck and ejects. Wendy and Graham tow him to shore.

Ben has one more caribou fence marked on his maps. We slither out of our kayaks on a stony beach below Canyon Creek. A narrow scree gully breaches the rock ramparts of the canyon. We clamber upwards. The sun shines brightly, but the air is pleasantly cool. And there are no mosquitoes.

Between the canyon walls and the foothills the land is flat, a piece of transplanted prairie. I walk towards the mountains and turn back. The canyon's ragged incision is neatly hidden. What is all-encompassing at water level is invisible from a few hundred meters away.

We walk through scattered stones, at first glance natural clusters. From the top of a nearby hill, a pattern emerges. The rocks had been piled to mimic people, or as cairns to support poles that helped funnel the caribou to waiting hunters.

We can see the pattern because many of the stones have been recently painted a vivid white. It is an accepted procedure to coat rocks with lime to aid aerial survey and photography. Lime washes away quickly, but here enterprising scientists have gone one better, selecting a durable enamel.

I sit among the stones, the only sound the sigh of the breeze in the willows. I try to imagine the indigenous people awaiting the arrival of the caribou. Modern biologists can't predict the time and route of the migration. How did these people, with so much more at stake, know where and when to make their preparations?

A familiar whine drowns out the songs of the land.

"You'd think we were in Vietnam," says Wendy angrily, looking up. The clatter builds to a crescendo as the helicopter flashes overhead, an audible reminder of how life has changed.

We climb Engigstciak, a solitary bluff twenty kilometers from the coast. The tundra below is a green carpet, dotted with ponds. The Firth, a tangled web of glistening threads, merges with the distant sea.

At least nine different native cultures have looked for game from Engigstciak's commanding summit. Spear tips, scrapers, blades, and bone awls indicate that the north slope has been inhabited for at least five thousand years.

Raptors have replaced human hunters as the prime users of this vantage point. Falcon scat spots the crown of Engigstciak's rocky head.

My eyes sweep the lowlands, hoping to catch sight of musk oxen. These shaggy animals are a throwback to hoary creatures that once roamed the north — wooly mammoths, bison, camels, and giant beavers all dwelt here. Musk oxen survived the climatic changes that killed off other mammal populations, but defensive postures that withstood thousands of years of predation and native hunting were of little avail against men with rifles. The native musk oxen that roamed Alaska and the Yukon were hunted to extinction by the late 1800s.

Nearing the Arctic Ocean.

A small herd has filtered back to the Yukon from Alaska, where they've been reintroduced.

Herschel Island's frozen mud banks brood off the Arctic Coast. A north wind has carried in pack ice. The bergs are ghost-like in a writhing mist, fantastic shapes rearing above the slate-colored water. Fog rolls in from the ocean, obscuring the island and chilling the air. We scramble down to our kayaks and paddle north into an insistent headwind.

The bird life changes as we near the sea. A whistling swan runs into the undergrowth, ducking its head. The rich plumages of golden plovers, phalaropes, and ruddy turnstones splash the shore with bright color. Kitelike tail feathers trail behind jaegers. Sandpipers explode into flight.

I drift below a hovering arctic tern. Its wings beat jerkily, tail spread wide. These birds undertake the longest migration of any living thing. The terns on the Firth have finished nesting, and are now building reserves of fat for their 20,000-kilometer journey south. Terns are a few grams of fluff on a thin frame — not what you'd call powerful flyers, but they've learned to take advantage of prevailing winds. They are literally blown to the Antarctic, where krill abounds in the icy waters.

The wind picks up. We stop for a snack behind a dune that creates the illusion of shelter. It isn't until we wrench our cramped bodies out of our cockpits that we realize how cold we were.

The raw, damp breeze blows through our sweat-soaked clothes. We hastily gather driftwood for a blazing fire. I shiver, even while crouched close to the flames. Dancing sparks threaten to sear holes in my dry suit, yet I am reluctant to wriggle out of its security. Hot drinks and a large meal barely keep hypothermia at bay.

We set up tents, forcing our numbed fingers to close around poles and pegs. I tumble into my sleeping bag wearing a toque and mitts.

Even the minute draught of our kayaks is too deep for the shoals at the mouth of the Firth. Our maiden taste of Arctic salt water isn't free floating. We wade with numbed feet and ankles.

A maroon sailboat is anchored in the shallow harbor of a sand spit, an unlikely spot to find a pleasure cruiser. The boat looks sturdy and serviceable. No frills. Neatly repaired scars near the waterline indicate clashes with icebergs. A young man wearing a black toque lowers himself into a punt tethered to the stern of the boat and rows towards us.

"Come aboard for a hot drink," he says.

The boat's captain is English, his crew from New Zealand. They'd travelled from the Atlantic the summer before, winding through the Arctic Archipelago to the Mackenzie Delta. The ship had been berthed in Inuvik for the winter. Now they are holed up, waiting for a shift in the wind that will blow the Beaufort ice out to sea.

"We've seen surprisingly few animals," says one of the Kiwis. "Seals, one polar bear, and some belugas, but no big whales."

Arctic tern.

    I grip a hot mug to warm my hands and reach for a cookie. We swap stories, each intrigued by the others' style of adventure. I can see them creeping along, mountains of ice rising on each flank, sudden storms heeling their boat in a screaming squall of horizontal spray.

    We thank them for their hospitality and climb into kayaks that seem tiny and frail compared to the sailboat. A tailwind whips up sizable waves and we surf towards Pauline Cove.

    Pauline Cove had been a bustling settlement during Herschel Island's whaling days. A few weathered wooden buildings still stand, alongside newer shelters built for a Yukon territorial park. Driftwood has been stacked to create a rudimentary wind shelter. We set up our tents on the sand.

    Fifteen vessels had sheltered here during the winter of 1894-1895, at the height of the whaling. By 1907, bowhead whales were close to extinction, and the whalers sailed for more fertile waters.

    A towering oil drilling rig squats in the cove. We can see another near the mainland, standing like a skyscraper. The colossal structures are lifeless, abandoned by exploration companies, waiting for the price of oil to rise.

January 1991

"We're willing to share the land," says Norma, "as long as they don't come to rape it, as long as they don't come to bulldoze it."

I think about the efforts I make to cut back on energy consumption. Walking into town, turning out the lights, planning to move to a smaller house... but still, I drive to the rivers, and I paddle a plastic kayak. "When you talk to people in the south," I ask, "what do you ask them to do to help?"

"Everyone has to do what they can," she says, staring at me with intense brown eyes. "In the near future, the oil is going to run out. The lights will go out in New York. The lights will go out in Winnipeg. Only the ones that are closest to the land will survive."

"In Old Crow, I don't need a car. I can go out at minus sixty. I can live in a tent." Her dark eyes are misted, tears are close to the surface. "But we need the caribou. I don't want to see my people go hungry. We'd die without the caribou."

"When this fight started, we began having meetings with all the Gwich'in, from the Yukon and Alaska. At the first meetings, some of the young people started talking about fighting, about violence. The elders stood up and told them to be quiet. But last time, not one elder said anything. Finally, an elder stood up, an old man, and he said that he too would fight for his land." She looks at me. "What else can they do?"

We stand up and pull the parkas from the back of our chairs. I pay the woman at the till for the coffee. I give her two one-dollar coins, coins with a swimming loon on one side. We walk into the lobby near the headless rack of caribou antlers, and I reach into my pack for my toque and mitts.

"When I was a little girl I had a favorite place near a lake," Norma says. "An elder once sat with me and said that some day there would be just one loon left out there. The ducks and geese and swans would be gone, and there would be just one loon. Now, when I go home, I go back and sit at the same place and look out. And all I can see are a couple of loons. I sit and look at those loons."

COAL RIVER

SAND IN MY SURPRISE PEAS

August 1989

My yellow raincoat hangs over my youngest daughter like a circus tent. She puts her arms through an orange life jacket and zips it up. The top of the raincoat is now squeezed in, but the bottom flares out like a square-dance dress. Red, drooping long underwear disappears into multicolored wool socks and soggy running shoes. It's a good thing her school friends can't see her now.

She kneels in the stern of the canoe, and pulls up the skirt of the spray cover. Everything is hidden but her arms, shoulders, and a worried face. I climb in and we wait in the eddy while Jody Schick and my other daughter Kirsten get into their boat. Wendy and my niece Katrina are standing on shore by their canoe, waiting to see how we make out in the rapid before launching.

Jody smiles cheerfully. I can see a mouthful of braces. Kirsten squints downstream, a thin horizontal line above her eyebrows. I grab their gunnel and we drift away together.

"We're going to back ferry to the left to avoid those shallow ledges," I say, "then paddle forward through that chute."

"All right Kirst," I yell, "gimme five."

"Yeah," she says with muted enthusiasm. We slap our hands together, but her eyes are still glued on the rapid.

"Okay Polly, as soon as we eddy out, start backpaddling."

I look back to see how Kirsten and Jody are doing. Kirsten looks grim. She's putting all her weight into a pry, all her fifty kilograms, but that's not much force to counteract the swift current. Jody is working hard, no braces visible between his lips. Each time they draw or pry to correct the angle of their ponderous canoe, the current whips them downstream. They're bearing down on us.

I watch the shrinking distance between our canoes nervously, and mistime our dash though the chute. "Paddle forward Polly!"

Our canoe scrapes an exposed chunk of bedrock and lurches into the chute at the wrong spot, at the wrong angle. The bow crunches into a ledge, whiplashing me forward onto a desperate low brace. The river is foaming past. We're at a full stop.

"Daddy," says a small voice, "I think I lost my paddle."

The black handle of the paddle bobs downstream. As I reach for it Kirsten and Jody's canoe slams alongside, knocking us free. I fling the paddle to Jody, who relays it to Polly.

Last year I kayaked the Coal River with a group of adult friends. I remember floating through these rapids, feeling free, watching the beads of water splash over my bow. It has been a few years since I led a group of teenagers down a river, but now the feeling of responsibility floods back. My insides start to knot.

July 1989

Before we leave for the Coal, we gather at the Yukon River to work on our canoeing skills.

It's been as hot a summer as anyone can remember. The sun is blasting down and only a few fluffy clouds are drifting carelessly in the sky. Some little kids are splashing each other in a big eddy. We're practising eddy turns.

Kirsten and Jody are floundering on the eddy line. "You don't want to get broadside in a canoe," I say. "It turns slowly, and you end up with five meters of boat heading towards the rocks."

"No way," laughs Jody. "I'm bringing my kayak instead." At the ripe age of fifteen, he is already an accomplished kayaker. He knows you can't depend on a canoe to behave the same way.

"Paddle forward," yells Wendy. "Lean the boat downstream. No, lean the *boat* downstream, catch the current with your paddle and lean out over it."

Katrina looks resigned, but patient. She went through this before, a couple of years ago, when she came up from Vancouver to see what life in the north was about. She lived with us for most of a year and was in the outdoor education class I taught at a local junior high school. The highlight of the course was a late spring canoe trip on the Big Salmon River. Now she is back up for a summer job, selling plastic Ninja Turtles under the fluorescent lights of a Whitehorse toy store.

"Okay Polly," I say, "let's switch sides. Now what stroke are you going to do?"

Kirsten and Jody practise their strokes.

August 1989

It's early evening when we drive into Watson Lake. At the edge of town there is a thicket of whitewashed poles, the "Signpost Forest." Row after row of motley signs are nailed to the posts.

"New York is big, but this is BIGGAR."

"Pottsville - Pop. 411." I wonder if the sheriff in Pottsville would drop the vandalism charge if he knew that the stolen sign would promote tourism in Watson Lake.

They say that it was started by a homesick soldier during the construction of the Alaska Highway. Now Winnebagos are attracted to the signposts, like ravens to a split garbage bag. Cameras click and bumper stickers read "We're spending our children's inheritance."

We don't stop. We turn left and drive to the float-plane dock, where three planes are bobbing on the lake, an Otter, a Cessna 185, and something smaller, something fragile looking. Jody has flown in small planes before, but it's the first time for Kirsten, Polly, and Katrina.

"Oh my god," says Polly quietly. "They're *small*."

We sleep in bumpy tent sites in the trees behind the office. Early in the morning, Wendy and Jody rattle off in the Sagwagon. They drive 160 kilometers west to the confluence of the Coal and Liard rivers. After he drops us off, the pilot will land on the Liard to pick them up with their canoe, and fly them back to join us. Our truck will be waiting for us at the end of the trip.

The pilot lashes two canoes to the pontoons of the Otter and we pass him our gear. I hunch over so I don't smash my head on the door, and wriggle into the front seat. The girls strap themselves into seats in the back and start whispering. Whispering so the pilot won't hear them.

"The ceiling's padded," says Kirsten.

"Your seat belts done up?" asks the pilot. He fiddles with switches, pulls a knob, pushes a button. The propeller twitches several times, then the engine roars with life. The plane starts to vibrate.

"Feel the sides," says Polly, "they're shaking."

"How old do you think this plane is?" asks Kirsten.

"Don't worry," Katrina answers, "*I'm* the one next to the door. What if it flies open?"

We taxi across the lake and turn into the wind. The pilot opens the throttle. At first we plow across the lake, plumes of water curling from the pontoons like breaking surf. Soon we skip across the waves and bounce into the air. When we're above the trees, the plane banks sharply and heads west.

I turn around and signal thumbs up. My daughters and niece are growing up, but for the moment they look young, sophistication drained from their faces along with most of the blood.

The roar of the engine makes talk impossible and we look out the windows. The Alaska Highway is a beige ribbon laid against the boreal forest. Billows of dust follow the traffic like jet streams. We veer away from the highway and fly over low wooded hills pockmarked with lakes. I see a moose standing in a shallow pond. From this angle it's a small brown blob with no legs. I gesture to the girls and they flatten their noses against the windows.

Last year, instead of flying, we had portaged between a series of lakes and grovelled down an overgrown creek that meandered to the river. We had slid our canoes over beaver dams, dragged them around log jams, carried them through the woods.

The creek is insignificant from the air. We flash over it and soon are circling over the river. It doesn't seem possible that we'd thrashed for a day and a half in such a tiny piece of the Yukon bush. Like looking through the wrong end of binoculars, speed distorts my feelings about the land.

I've been reading *Islandia*, an early twentieth-century Utopian novel full of questions about the merits of "progress." Last night I read about the ski trip that Don, an Islandian adventurer, and John Lang, disillusioned American consul, took across a high pass. Islandian people had buffered themselves from modern technology, preferring the old ways, preferring to ride horses rather than trains, preferring to walk or ski rather than drive a car.

Trying to sleep in a high hut while the mountains cracked with the cold, Don asked John Lang about life in America:

He asked me a number of curious questions about the United States. Do not trains and swift boats and automobiles change one's feelings about the size of the country? Do they not alter one's interest in natural things?

I remember, almost a decade ago, arriving at Virginia Falls. We had just finished three weeks of slow travel: one week of lugging our gear upriver from the upper South MacMillan River to the headwaters of the Nahanni, two weeks of moving with the river currents and exploring by foot.

There were several other parties at the falls. A float plane droned overhead, bringing a woman and a teenage girl for an afternoon visit to this World Heritage Site. The woman was wearing a polyester suit and carrying a purse. The girl trailed after her, her white sandals dusty from the trail. "It's okay here," she said, "but these little trees are *so ugly*."

The plane drops us off on a small lake, takes off, and soon returns with Wendy, Jody, and our third canoe. The lake is connected to the Coal River by the final section of the creek we'd slithered down last year. We have no beaver dams to ski jump, but our path to the river is still blocked by log jams and uprooted trees. The canoes stubbornly catch on protruding branches and roots, obstinate as mules. We try to stay dry at first, but realize the futility and soon are standing thigh deep in the stream, lifting and prodding.

After we've been out for a few days, the physical aspect of travel will become part of our life, as simple and automatic as brushing our teeth. Now though, fresh out of the airplane, our pace seems too slow, our effort too demanding.

"How *far* is it to the river?" asks Polly.

In the late summer, where the creek mingles with the Coal, a gravel bar is exposed. We carry our gear across the wet sand and rocks and up a small embankment, where, concealed by a screen of trees, there is a level clearing of hard-packed sand. While Wendy puts up a tent, I carry the food bags away from the boats and dig around until I find the bagels, cheese, and fresh fruit we've brought for the first lunch.

Tent sites beside the Coal River.

"Where are we going to put up our tent?" asks Polly.

"Wherever you like," I say.

"It doesn't matter," calls out Jody, "I already have the most awesome site."

"No way," yells Kirsten, "look at this spot. It's the best."

"Hurry up with your tent," I say, "so we can look for the springs."

I've heard about the Coal River springs from Ben Moise, and looked at his slides of the tufa formations, caused by calcium precipitating from the water. An X marking the springs is only a few centimeters upstream on my map, on the other side of the Coal.

We decide to line our canoes upriver, something I haven't done since the Nahanni. I quickly discover that normal length bow and stern ropes just don't work for upstream tracking.

"Try to keep the bow angled just slightly into the current," I say. But the canoe obstinately edges into shore, grounding on rocks and gravel. Polly kicks it back into the current, but I pull too hard on my rope and again it noses into the beach.

"It's easier just wading and pushing it," says Polly.

Wendy, Jody and I have been on a succession of wilderness trips this summer, and are quickly absorbed by the rhythms of the land: a tiny spring with crystal water dripping through moss, the sound of the river splashing over shallows, the gray blur of a dipper flying just above the water.

The girls, however, are still marching to a more mechanized beat. Their unused muscles clamor for attention. They're trying, but are grim-faced, not yet confident of their strengths and limits.

"What about a rest?" asks Wendy. We splay out on boulders and I take the gummy bear candies out of my day pack.

"Are you sure you know where these springs are?" asks Kirsten.

The river is deep and slow where it slices through the rock walls. We're able to paddle faster than the gentle current and we inch upstream to a gravel beach. We pull up the canoes, turn them over, and start walking. I wonder how we'll know when to turn inland, but a gushing stream of water is a clue too obvious to miss. A bright, unnatural-looking wall reflects the sunlight through a band of trees.

The air is heavily scented. We come to a swampy meadow covered with knee-high wild mint. Behind it are rounded, bulging tiers of tufa, sculptured through hundreds of years of patient dripping. A creek of spring water flows before the walls, like a moat in front of a castle, with a fallen log for a draw-bridge.

To get to the log, we skirt the edge of the lush forest. My running shoes are already wet, so I step into the creek to bypass a patch of prickly wild roses. My foot sinks in a patch of mud that grips like quicksand.

"Yuuck," I yell. "Gross."

I retrieve my foot with a slurping burp, but my shoe is mired. I grab Jody's arm for support and I grope in the muck. The girls are pointing and laughing. "I wouldn't step here," I say.

Tufa.

We walk across the log. There is an easy route up the tufa, which looks tough, like concrete, but is actually fragile and easily crushed underfoot. It takes centuries to rebuild after being trampled upon.

"Don't walk on the tufa," yells Wendy. We scramble through the undergrowth instead. At the top, the spring splashes through a luxuriant growth of moss and monkey flowers. The tiers are formed by a series of distinct pools, each with crimped edges, like the borders on fancy birthday cakes. Blooms of algae tint the water with bright, unreal greens.

"Man . . . ," says Jody.

"Amazing," agrees Wendy.

We all try out adjectives, but words are inadequate and our comments dribble into silence. We stay at the springs until hunger drives us back to our canoes. The banks that we had struggled by a few hours earlier drift past in a few minutes of free floating.

It's late August and the mosquitos have disappeared. Pockets of blackflies emerge in the late summer and fall in the Yukon, but there aren't enough here to bother me. I lean against a tree after supper and flip open *Islandia*. I'm with John Lang, riding his horse along a dusty trail, when a screech brings me suddenly back to the Coal River.

"Polly, watch out! You're getting sand all over my clothes."

I notice the dome tent quiver violently.

"I'm making sure there aren't any spiders in my sleeping bag."

"Well, shake it outside," counters Kirsten.

"We'd better look under the packs," says Polly.

"Remember that huge millipede we saw in Yosemite?" says Kirsten, "Did anyone check in the corner where *my* head is going to be?"

"We searched for bugs already, when we set up the tent."

"Fine. But I bet one crawled into your sleeping bag when we were at the springs."

The conversation stops for a while, although the sides of the tent still shake. I get back to *Islandia*.

"I'm not sleeping in the middle. It's too hot and squishy."

"*Katrina*," says Polly. "You said you wanted it."

"I was in the middle last night in Watson Lake, so I get the side nearest the river."

"Okay, fine... that's where the bears will come first."

"No way! They'll come out of the bush."

"You guys," yells Kirsten, "I'm trying to read."

The light fades and it's too dark to read. Faint stars gleam between the clouds that are sailing overhead, I can see the scoop of the Big Dipper, and Polaris. I haven't seen stars since the bounding increase of daylight in the spring quenched their fire. I welcome them back like old friends who went south for the summer.

Wendy has already zipped our sleeping bags together. I crawl in and worm over to her side.

"Hey," she says indignantly, " keep your feet away from my warm stomach."

I can still hear muffled voices from the dome tent.

"Kirsten. I have to go to the bathroom. Come with me."

"*Polly!* I just got warm."

"Come on Kirsten, I forgot to go earlier."

"Oh, all right."

I wake up clear-headed. Something is splashing in the river. Something heavy. I unzip the tent fly and stick my head and shoulders into the night.

"What is it?" asks Wendy.

Northern lights sweep across the sky. I can see it now, a black silhouette against the dull gleam of highlights on the water.

"It's a moose." It clatters across the gravel bar and the sounds of breaking branches recede in the night. I squirm back into the sleeping bag.

Bull moose.

It's light outside, but the sun isn't up when I hear more splashing. This time I feel groggy as I poke my head into the cool air. A cow moose with a calf are wading towards us across the river.

"Hey Kirsten, Polly, Katrina," I call. "Hey Jody."

"What?" answers Jody in a sleepy voice.

"Look down at the river."

"What's happening?" mumbles Kirsten.

"Come over here," I say.

They stumble out of their tents. The cow and calf are standing still in midriver, the rushing river gurgling around their knees. Everyone crowds around our tent, looking down at the moose. The calf waits until its mother starts to move, then follows her through the shallows, across the gravel bar and into the forest.

I get up to make coffee. The girls crawl back into their sleeping bags, but Jody sits down and we talk about kayaking.

I was hoping for an early start, but I'd forgotten how long it takes inexperienced people to pack up. I'm used to stuffing sleeping bags as as I get up, to cooking breakfast while Wendy dismantles the tent, to carrying loads to the boats as soon as they are ready.

Now Kirsten is brushing her hair, and Polly and Katrina are standing around awkwardly, waiting for her to finish before they do anything.

I can see dozens of things that they need to do and I feel irritated. I bite my tongue, because I know that I shouldn't force my agenda upon them. We don't *have* to leave early. I open *Islandia* and lean against a log. Jody carries his last load to the canoes and comes back carrying his book, *The Stainless Steel Rat*.

"Katrina," yells Kirsten, "you haven't rolled your sleeping-pad yet."

"I know Kirsten, I have to go to the bathroom."

"Polly, is this your sock?"

I put down my book and walk over. The tent is unzipped, the door and mosquito netting squashed into the fine sand. A black backpack is lying on the zipper, grinding it further.

"Hey," I say, "this is a fast way to ruin a zipper." I pick it up, shake it, brush it off, and lay it inside the tent. "Try to keep it off the ground."

I go back to my book, and a while later their stuff is down by the boats. I walk around camp to make sure that we haven't left any junk behind. At the girl's tent-site I find a nearly transparent candy wrapper and a green twist-tie under the seed pods of a lupine.

Down at the canoes, I pull out them out. "I found these where your tent was," I say. "You have to search more carefully."

"We did look," says Kirsten with the beginnings of a frown.

I'm trying to show my love of the land by my actions, but I find myself nagging, and I don't feel good about it.

Waterfalls tumble into the Coal River.

The next morning, floating with the current, it seems that we are still, that the banks are flowing upriver. A row of trees beside the Coal blocks our view of clearings, of wildlife, of hills. We only catch occasional glimpses of what lies within the forest, like flashes of a living room through the curtains from a dark street. It's only when we pull over for a snack, or to camp, that we get a closer look.

From the canoe, we look sideways, or up. It's natural to gaze downwards when our feet are again on land. The forest is quiet, but animal tracks tell that it isn't always so. A wolf has been on this gravel bar in the last couple of days, as well as several moose. A web of tiny tracks is impossible for me to read. Mice? Voles? Shrews?

The forest floor is a carpet of caribou moss — pale lichen and moss that is damp, soft, and springy from recent rain. There is a pile of gnawed cones under a spruce. I hear a squirrel chattering in the distance, but the one responsible for the shredded cones is quiet. We push the boats back into the water and continue on.

The river is calm, but the current is strong. Jody grabs our stern, and I stick one leg into Katrina and Wendy's canoe. We drift together and share some crackers, cheese, and dried fruit.

"What are those ducks?" asks Kirsten.

Ahead of the canoes are a dozen low-slung gray ducks. They congregate near shore, swimming back and forth nervously, heads moving from side to side like those of spectators at a tennis match. We steer to the opposite shore, to sneak past, to leave them in peace. But as we come abreast, the ducks clatter downstream in a flurry of wing beats and running webbed feet.

"Mergansers," I say. "We'll see them again, around the corner. I once followed a bunch all day on the Dease River."

"Can I see the map?" asks Kirsten.

I pass it across and lay back. The sun is warm and I feel lazy. The only sounds are the rasping of the gunnels, and splashes of water between the canoes.

"What about these waterfalls?" asks Kirsten, jabbing her finger towards the canyon section of the river.

I sit up. "The map is screwed. Last year we kept looking for horizon lines on the river . . . there are a couple of hard rapids at the end of the canyon, but no falls."

We paddle and float through that day and the next. Ravens fly overhead, in straight lines; hawks circle with high-pitched wails. We stop to explore a side-creek that tumbles down a limestone face riddled with caves. Dusk approaches. A beaver ferries out towards us and dives with a loud "thwack" of its tail. We watch to see where it will surface, but it doesn't appear again.

We camp just above the first rapids in the Coal's canyon. Rock walls downstream remind me of the canyons below Virginia Falls on the Nahanni, which are, as the raven flies, less than two hundred kilometers to the east.

Behind the ribbon of sand where we perch our tents is a steep forested hillside tangled with deadfall. A heart-shaped waterfall foams into the river, sliding down a rock slab. Next to it is a dripping rock wall, lined with golden streaks of tufa.

Jody squats near a pile of driftwood beside the river and soon blue smoke spirals up. He balances our small grate over the fire and fills a pot for tea. The sun is long gone, and the air has the sharp chill of autumn. Kirsten rummages in the food bags.

"Polly, let's wash our hair," says Katrina.

"Okay."

"Why don't you wait until tomorrow when the sun comes out?" I ask. I've just put on a toque, and I can't imagine dunking my head in the river.

"No way," says Polly, "My hair is *so* greasy. I need to wash it now."

"Well . . . don't rinse the suds in the river."

"Why can't we?" They look offended. "It's biodegradable."

"Even biodegradable soap affects the river," I answer. "Rinse the suds out on the ground, way back from the river."

They don't look happy about it, but they take the big pot and walk to the other end of the sand bar. I'm used to being completely relaxed on the river, but now I feel tense. I don't like being the Grinch that stole the fun from the canoe trip, but I can't help my enviromania. I used to use shampoo on river trips, too, but now I don't mind my hair hanging in dreadlocks until we reach a hot shower.

Katrina stands over Polly with a bucket of river water and starts to pour. "Katrina, not all over my sweater!"

Kirsten writes her impression of the camp at the start of the canyon.

Our tents were perched on a ribbon of sand near the edge of the canyon. A waterfall cascaded past mottled orange walls high above us. A towering beacon of rock marked the start of the first rapids. The last twilight faded and a few stars poked out. There was no wind to stir the crisp autumn air.

My mood, however, was anything but tranquil. After two days of mellow paddling, pounding rapids were the last thing I wanted to hear. Jody, Wendy, and my dad lay in the sand, reading. Even Jody, who was usually too active to read, had his nose in The Stainless Steel Rat. Sure that they eagerly anticipated tomorrow's whitewater, I hesitated to admit my nervousness.

Ironically, it was my night to make dinner. I felt that my stomach had been left somewhere upstream where the river was calmer. Stirring the pasta slowly, I imagined possible outcomes of tomorrow's paddle. I saw myself paralyzed in the bow of the canoe as we headed towards a huge hole; I saw myself knocking Jody unconscious with my paddle as we slammed into a rock; I saw myself becoming hopelessly tangled in the spray deck as we tipped, being dragged downwards . . .

"Look Kirsten," said Polly. "I'll help you with the peas, okay? We're starving." She and Katrina bent over the pot of Surprise peas, watching them grow from shrivelled lumps into plump green blobs.

Hunger aside, we had had some problems adjusting to the wilderness. We knew that the exacting standards my dad outlined for keeping the back country untouched were important . . . but it was easy to forget, leaving hair elastics scattered in the rush to vacate a campsite, or accidentally throwing foil wrappers on the fire. The short lectures he delivered were informing, but made me feel inadequate . . . river etiquette that is second nature to them seems alien to someone who has travelled little in the outdoors.

The noodles came to a boil and I scooped them into bowls and two-cupper mugs. Katrina gave the Surprise peas a final stir.

"Katrina," yelled Wendy, "is this your shampoo bottle floating in the eddy?"

Katrina stood up. Her foot just nicked the brimming pot, but it was enough. The shaky iron grate collapsed. Peas cascaded into the sand, peas escaped in a rush to the river, peas sank in the eddy.

"Uh-oh." Polly looked worried, but a giggle was dangerously close to the surface. My dad appeared on the scene. He watched the peas bobbing merrily towards the rapids, his face decidedly grim.

"Well . . . we better clean this up," he said as he bent down towards the river, scooping a large handful of sandy pea soup. His body language radiated disapproval. Our mirth disappeared as we bent to the task of separating the soft green spheres from the sticky sand.

"It was an accident," said Wendy.

My dad relaxed slightly, "Well, so much for vegetables for dinner."

We captured some of the renegade peas, but many escaped to ride through the very rapids which I viewed with such trepidation.

Meal preparation.

The pea episode leaves me mad at myself. I know it's no big deal. I know the peas will wash away and decompose. It's as though I'm a marionette, jerking each time someone pulls an environmental string. One of the strings is "Don't leave extra food behind that will disrupt wild creatures." The lesson could be learned without a lecture, but I react without thinking.

The river flows past us, bends right around a huge boulder, and funnels into a dark rushing tongue. A pale yellow bar of light across the western horizon reflects ghostly impressions of the rapid. Soon the campfire illuminates a narrow radius, a rocky shelf, the beach, and dark water lapping below the canoes. The rapid is a muted echo from tufa-coated walls.

Coal canyon.

The next morning the sun shines and the rapids don't seem too intimidating. We paddle through a succession of rapids, stopping now and again to explore the canyon. In the early afternoon we land at a beach that is made for camping. We were a tightly knit group in the whitewater, but now we disperse to do our own things. I wander off with my camera for a few hours, come back, and trade it for my book. I lean against the trunk of an unusually large spruce and try to get into *Islandia*, but it's hard to imagine another Utopia when you are in one.

"Jody," says Kirsten, "it says on the package that these noodles will feed twelve."

"Oh man," he replies. "They're already in the water."

He stirs the tomato sauce that he had dried before the trip. Then he walks over to his food bag and pulls out half a dozen green bananas, half a dozen hard green bananas. "I bought green ones so they wouldn't squish." He puts each on a rectangle of tin foil and throws in handfuls of chocolate chips and marshmallows. "They'll soften up as they cook," he says hopefully.

Alpenglow shimmers in shades of gold on the eastern walls of the canyon, turning pink as the light fades. I look over at the dome tent, under a cottonwood tree. They must have finished their insect check because Polly is brushing her hair, talking with Katrina. Wendy walks past the overturned canoes, her face and arms pink and glowing from a cold bath.

I look over at Jody and Kirsten, squatting near the fire. A castle-shaped chunk of bedrock sits in the center of the river just downstream. The left side of the river drops over a ledge: on the right it is constricted, throwing up a train of irregular standing waves.

"Supper's ready," yells Jody.

The big pot is a writhing mass of noodles. Filling our mugs doesn't seem to deplete the pasta.

"Save some room for banana boats," says Jody. He grabs a piece of driftwood and fishes around in the fire. He flips a charred chunk of tin foil onto the sand. The chocolate and marshmallow ooze and flow together, but the banana looks petrified. I reach for another helping of spaghetti.

After four days on the river we should be feeling confident, but the rapids we face the next morning are difficult. We run a couple successfully, then stop to look at a maze of ledges and exposed bedrock. We scout from shore, mapping out complex sequences of moves. Polly, standing on a rock in my oversized yellow raincoat, looks nervous.

"I'd like to watch to see how you do," says Wendy.

"We'll follow you, Daddy," says Kirsten.

"Give us about ten seconds before you start," I say.

We get into our canoes and drift away together. "We're going to back ferry to the left to avoid those shallow ledges," I say, "then paddle forward through that chute."

Kirsten looks worried so I try to lighten the mood. "Hey Kirst," I yell, "gimme five."

Polly and I plow into the downstream current. Kirsten and Jody, who want to copy our maneuvers, ignore the ten-second interval and follow closely.

"Pry Kirsten!" says Jody, "We're losing our angle."

"Jody, Jody . . . they're not moving."

"Just keep prying."

"We're going to ram them!"

"Back paddle harder, Kirsten."

"There's a rock on the left. Draw! No wait, pry!" yells Kirsten

"They tipped," Jody shouts. "No they didn't . . . but they're stuck."

"What do we do?"

"Just don't do what they did. Paddle forward!"

They ricochet off us and jar us free. I toss Polly's paddle to Jody, and he flings it to her. We float into calm water. I try to act calm, I don't want to make anyone nervous, but my forehead feels tight with strain. The rest are watching Wendy and Katrina, but I'm looking downstream.

The next rapid is the longest and most complicated yet, but we weave through the ledges with precision and style.

"Well done," I tell the others in the next eddy. "Just like ballet on the water!"

"Right," says Kirsten, "more like a kindergarten Christmas concert."

"At least we made it," I say. "This next one looks easy."

The river is broad and shallow. We back ferry across the river to a chute wide enough for an eighteen-wheeler. I'm feeling more relaxed, and I don't pay attention to the current lines.

"Okay Polly, we can paddle forward now."

A horizontal ledge redirects some of the current almost perpendicular to the rest of the downstream flow. Instead of paddling into the tongue, we lurch towards an insignificant-looking hole. I lean downstream to brace. The canoe hits the underlying bedrock. It sticks.

Polly watches me brace, watches the boat tilt at a crazy angle, watches me struggling out of the loose folds of the spray cover. Everything is happening in slow motion, and she doesn't yet realize that we're going over. The cold hits like an afterthought.

"Polly," I yell, "are you all right?"

"Yes . . . and I've got my paddle!"

"Stay on the upstream end of the canoe," I say, grabbing the rope and swimming towards shore. There is nothing to worry about downstream, but the waterlogged boat weighs a tonne. It follows reluctantly.

Wendy and Katrina riding waves.

Kirsten and Jody's boat cuts into view. From water level it looks like the prow of a ship, the faces look small and white. "Are you okay?" asks Jody.

"Couldn't be better," I say, grabbing their stern painter. "Paddle for shore!"

Soon my arms are stretched as though I'm a bungee cord, but the bank is coming nearer. "Don't try to stand until we're next to shore," I yell to Polly. Wendy and Katrina nudge our boat with theirs, and in a couple of minutes we're on land, shivering and dripping.

I pop the snaps on the spray deck and we drain the canoe. Our gear survived the dunking and we pull on dry long underwear and sweaters.

"Are you warm enough?" asks Wendy. "Maybe we should light a fire."

Thin sunshine penetrates the wispy overcast, enough warmth for at least moral support. "I'm fine," says Polly and I agree. We get back in the canoes.

The next rapid is another labyrinth of rocks and ledges. The only route is on the right, but a cliff hugs the shore and we have to scout from a sand bar on the opposite side.

"I'm sure there's a route over there," I say, peering across the wide river.

Polly is quiet. She looks nervous. I try to make light of the rapid by putting on my best bluff and hearty manner.

"Okay, Polly," I say, "let's do it!"

"We'll come after you," says Wendy.

We pick our way down, backpaddling from side to side, moving like a typewriter carriage. I can hear Wendy, not far behind.

"Pry, Katrina . . . there's another ledge . . . backpaddle hard . . . pry!"

I hear the crunch of boat against rock, but I'm too busy to look back until we're safely in the eddy below the rapid. Their canoe is upside down, beached on a shoal. Katrina picks herself out of the shallow water and stands on a rock. Wendy is tugging at the boat. Kirsten and Jody sail past, too intent on the whitewater to waste words of sympathy.

I hop from rock to rock, wade past a small rock wall, and slosh over to Wendy and Katrina. They're soaked from struggling out from the spray cover, but more embarrassed than upset.

"That was really stupid," says Wendy.

Katrina wades down to join the others while Wendy and I float the canoe downstream. We burrow into our diminishing supply of dry clothes and nibble on chocolate.

"How many more rapids are there?" asks Polly.

"Just a couple," I answer, "the two hardest ones." Her face falls and I quickly add, "Don't worry, they're easy to portage if you don't want to run them."

We climb out of our canoes to scout the first, a twisting rapid in a tight gorge. The cloud has thickened, a thick gray crust that blocks the sun. Wendy shivers and walks stiffly back to her canoe. She pulls out a toque and rain jacket.

"Look at that hole!" says Jody. "I wish I had my kayak."

"How would you run it in a canoe?" I ask.

He stares at the rapid, at the hole that guards the main tongue, at the cross waves that bounce off the rock walls, at the boils near the bottom of the gorge. "Um . . . I don't know."

The girls are looking at the rapid glumly. Wendy walks over, "I'm too cold to run it," she says. "I just don't want to swim again."

"I don't want to either," says Kirsten.

"Me either," agrees Polly, then Katrina.

"What do you think?" I ask Jody.

"Right on!"

We unload one canoe, carry it across the shelves of rock, and lower it into the pool below the rapid. Kirsten and Polly get in to rescue us in case we flip. Wendy and Katrina hold throw ropes. Jody and I walk back, pointing at the rapid and discussing tactics. We decide to power through the edge of the hole, then brace though the boils. It works.

At the final rapid there are two bedrock islands that split the river into three chutes. I want to take some pictures. I set up the tripod, and put the throw rope under it. We carry a rescue boat through a chimney between a cliff and a huge slab of bedrock, a fourth chute when the river is booming with spring floods. Katrina and Kirsten wait in the rescue canoe.

I hope my nagging hasn't tainted something precious.

Wendy and Jody plunge over the drop and slice through the hole without tipping. Katrina clambers out of the rescue boat, looking nervous, but decides to run the last canoe through with Wendy. Their expressions change from intent nervousness as they backpaddle to line up, to smiles of exhilaration as they come through unscathed.

"All right!" says Katrina.

"I thought you'd tip for sure," says Kirsten.

"It looked scary," adds Polly.

Jody looks over at me. "Man, I wish I had my kayak . . . I could get a great ender in that last hole," he says with a flash of braces.

We're all chilled, and we paddle steadily to warm up. Now that we're out of the canyon, now that we're nearing the Alaska Highway, my feelings of responsibility evaporate. I hope my nagging hasn't tainted something precious. I hope the kids remember the tufa, the moose, the river. I hope their memories make them want to preserve the fast-vanishing wilderness.

SNAKE RIVER

OTTERS AT $19.00

September 1981 - Mayo, Yukon

I arrive in Mayo on Labor Day for a year of teaching in a remote Yukon community, for a year of single fatherhood. I hold hands with my two young daughters and walk down the ramp of an ancient DC-3 into cool autumn sunshine.

For the past three years I had worked at the Outward Bound School in British Columbia, and travelled each winter. Now, the principal at J. V. Clark School seems like a turnkey. The twelve grade one and two students in my class have attention spans measured in milliseconds. Active.

I don't own a car, so Kirsten, Polly, and I walk everywhere. Before winter sets in, we wander through the spruce forest to skip stones on the Mayo River, along the way picking bagfuls of high-bush cranberries. We smell the berries long before we can see them, the forest saturated with cranberry perfume.

After Christmas, an Arctic cold front takes up residence in the central Yukon. During the next month, the mercury hovers near forty-five below, at times dipping to the mid-fifties. I swathe Polly in layers of leggings and sweaters and jam her into a snowsuit. It's such a tight squeeze that her elbows and knees don't bend. She walks stiff-legged to school in the morning, moving like a tiny Frankenstein's monster. The shiny outer layer of her snowsuit creaks in the cold.

"Polly," yells Kirsten, "can't you walk faster?"

Kirsten swears that one forty-below afternoon, I sent her down to Danny's Department Store to buy Tabasco sauce for my pizza, a skinny nine-year-old braving the ice fog. I don't remember.

Even before I came, I knew that I'd only stay for one school year. The winter is too long and my friends are too far away. The Stewart River is big and silty and slow moving and my kayak is in a garage three thousand kilometers to the south. There are no granite walls to climb, and even if there were, there is no one to climb them with.

If you plotted my movements on a map, you would see a small circle with ragged edges, a circle surrounded by wilderness. I know the wild land is there, but I only catch glimpses of it. A solitary fox often watches when I run out of town in the early morning, and once I think I hear wolves howling. This is an isolated northern community, but I'm insulated from the land, stuck in town by a web of responsibilities.

The locals are friendly, but reserved. I'm an outsider, bobbing along on the surface of social life like a stick of driftwood. I don't have the patience to sink below the surface to gain acceptance. I could have a few drinks and blend with the men at a Super Bowl party. Instead, I sit in the corner with my knitting needles and skeins of brightly colored wool. When someone asks, "Got your moose yet?" I reply, "I don't eat meat, much less shoot it."

Kirsten and Polly in Mayo, 1981.

August 1986 - Mayo and Snake River, Yukon

A plume of dust follows the Sagwagon out of Mayo. Our shuttle driver is returning to Whitehorse after dropping off Rachel, Graham, Wendy, and I. Tracee, Keith, Sandy, and Lois will come up for their flight tomorrow morning.

This is my first trip to Mayo since I hitched a ride south four years ago, the day school got out. I wander around town, looking at the school and the trailer where my kids and I lived. Danny's Department Store looks unchanged. I could walk through the door blindfolded, turn right, and lay my hands on brown-edged iceberg lettuce at $2.50 a head — 1981 prices.

I see a few familiar faces, but I don't know them well enough to talk about old times. The wilderness and wild animals are still just outside of town, but still unknown. I have the feeling that there is something I've lost, before I had the chance to find out what it was. I hope that on the Snake River I'll learn something about my companions, something about the land, and something about myself.

The moored Single Otter floats on a sweeping bend of the Stewart River. Several stony-faced old-timers loiter at a picnic table on a grassy embankment. They watch impassively as we carry the canoes and packs to the dock.

"I wonder where the pilot is?" asks Wendy.

Rachel and I walk over to the grass. Three kids and a scruffy husky run across the dirt road to see what's happening. They stand still for a moment, staring at me with round brown eyes. They're too young to be ex-students of mine.

"Do any of you know where the pilot is?" I ask.

The kids shake their heads, but one of the men gestures towards a squat hotel painted an uninspiring olive green.

"I'll see if I can find him," says Rachel.

In a few minutes a young man in jeans follows Rachel out of the hotel. He yawns. One side of his face is blotched with pillow marks.

"The flying has been crazy," he says, "but I need the money for university next winter. I have to grab catnaps when I can."

As our pilot lashes the canoes to the pontoons, a party of eight canoeists drives up, ready to fly to the headwaters of the Wind River. Emptying the queue would keep the pilot buzzing from noon until past midnight. Bush pilots aren't governed by the rigid flying restrictions of their cousins in commercial jets.

A couple of days after our uneventful flight to the headwaters of the Snake River, the same pilot slammed the Otter into the side of a ridge in the Selwyn Mountains. Fortunately, no one was injured, although the plane was a write-off.

Our tents are pitched above Duo Lakes, the closest spot to the upper Snake where a float plane can land. I can see the gravel wash of the river about a kilometer away. Between us and moving water is a sea of head-high willows. Showers have cleansed the air and the horizons are sharply focussed. The ridges are painted with washes of red and maroon. Bands of rock have eroded into scree slopes that look like huge brush strokes of color.

Wendy, Rachel, and I walk north on a gently inclined bench between the river valley and the alpine, picking our way between grassy clearings in the willows. On the hillside, two brown patches pick themselves up from among the rocks and look towards us.

"Caribou," I say.

"Wow," says Wendy, "they're the first I've ever seen."

"Me too," says Rachel.

The caribou traverse upwards, moving slowly, stopping to browse. We watch for a few minutes, then look for the next clearing. Wendy suddenly realizes that, if a grizzly was wandering through the willows, we would never see it.

"Hello bears," she yells. "Coming through, bears!"

"One of the best things about the wilderness," I say, "is the silence."

"*Ken!* You're supposed to let bears know you're around. Hell-ooo bears!"

The ground becomes rocky and we leave the bushes behind. Now we can see the glistening threads of the Snake flowing north. The dikelike barrier of an old rock slide thrusts towards the river, looking massive even from kilometers away. The bench drops away in front of us, into a rocky niche with a small lake.

"I'm going to head back to start making supper," says Wendy. She vanishes into the willows. "Hello bears . . ."

November 1990 - Whitehorse

Summer seems an impossible dream, like Christmas that refused to come when I was a kid. I'm in front of the computer, trying to write a magazine article about the Alsek River, but the words just aren't flowing. On days like today it's best to distract myself, so I flick on the radio and walk into the kitchen to make bread.

I listen to the news, the weather, the sports. I tip the dough onto the counter, throw a handful of flour on top, and begin kneading. I rock back on my heels, and then forward, finding a soothing rhythm.

"It's time for community announcements," says the radio host.

I wish I'd put a tape on instead, but it's too late, my hands are sticky and powdered with whole-wheat flour.

"The Yukon Fish and Game Club will be holding its Big Bull Night tonight at the Gold Rush Inn."

"Jesus," I think, "Big Bull Night."

"Bring in big game animals taken during the last season . . ."

"Great," I think, "another euphemism. Animals are never killed. They're *taken*, or *harvested*."

"Remember, bring your trophies and your stories — it's Big Bull night . . . families are welcome."

August 1986 - Snake River

"Coming hiking?" asks Tracee.

"I think I'll give my back a rest," I answer. I injured my back in the spring, kayaking in California, and I've been walking like an old man all trip.

"I'll stay with you," says Wendy.

Our friends shoulder day packs and disappear into the trees. I lie on my back in the warm sand, doing pelvic tilts. "Hey Ken," yells Wendy, "come here."

I roll to my knees and arthritically stand up. I walk up a hill behind camp to where Wendy is squatting. "Look at these blueberries!" she says.

Berries hang from the bushes like ornaments from a Christmas tree. We gorge ourselves, then circle upwards, filling lunch bags. Later, I press oily pastry into dutch ovens while Wendy makes a topping from granola, oats, sugar, and margarine. With two branches held like chopsticks, I transfer coals from the fire to the tops of the pots.

The blueberry pies are cooling when the others return.

"The hike was fantastic," says Lois.

"Incredible," agrees Keith.

"Let's go up there tomorrow morning," says Wendy. "If we leave early, we can start paddling in the afternoon."

Ptarmigan.

I wake up to a flat, gray light and prod Wendy. "It's morning," I say.

Our rustlings wake Rachel. She can't get back to sleep and crawls out of her tent. Keith and Graham had stayed up late around the fire, and embers glow when Rachel pokes them with a piece of driftwood. She piles twigs onto the coals, and blows them into crackling life.

You need to take advantage of those times you get up before your friends; it's an opportunity to collect "holier-than-thou" bonus points. Rachel stokes the fire and brews coffee. She carries mugs to Lois and Sandy's tent. "Here's some coffee!" she calls cheerfully and sets them down.

"Coffee's ready!" she tells the others.

Lois, Sandy, and Tracee stolidly ignore the steaming aroma from the mugs, but Keith and Graham are seduced from their sleeping bags. They sit in the quickening light, mugs of strong coffee held like crosses against the vampires of early morning. After some desultory conversation, the caffeine drives away the immediate desire for sleep.

"I wonder what time it is," says Keith. He unearths the only watch along on our trip. "Man! It's only five o'clock!" Rachel is buried with a torrent of abuse and achieves instant martyrdom.

Wendy and I climb through the spruce, which thin out as we gain elevation. We scramble upward through low-lying heather and alpine flowers. Ptarmigan flush out from under our feet, invisible until they explode upward. In flight, their vivid white belly feathers glow beneath their mottled upper bodies.

We walk up a game trail beaten into the spine of a ridge. A bull caribou ambles over a rise, stops on the path, and stares towards us. Its antlers, fully grown but still swathed in velvet, curl upward like slender grasping arms. It throws its head back and trots over the crest into the valley to the west.

We scramble to a col. "Let's stop for a snack," suggests Wendy.

I sit on a rock mottled with orange and white splashes of lichen. Wendy tosses me a bag of nuts and raisins. As I dig my hand into the bag, I notice movement below us. A dozen Dall sheep traverse a scree slope. The ewes walk sedately, but the lambs caper, exactly as lambs are supposed to.

We hike east along a ridge. We're quiet, wanting to maintain the spell. Ground squirrels stand like sentries, chattering and diving into holes as we pass. In the folds between spurs that radiate down to the river are lush glens. Twenty cow caribou and a few calves are grazing just below us. Three big bulls walk to the shelter of a huge overhanging boulder and lie down heavily.

In the afternoon, we eat a late lunch and pack the canoes. Until now, our river trip has been mainly wandering in the mountains, with only intermittent canoeing. We need to put some time on the water, but only a few kilometers downstream an appealing creek spills into the Snake. There is a broad gravelly beach with patches of sand and a backdrop of peaks. We know from topo maps that the river will soon flow into the Peel Valley, leaving the mountains behind.

"What do you think?" asks Sandy.

"I like it," says Wendy.

We set up camp and I try to stretch out my back, stiff from the hike. Graham collects driftwood. Keith borrows Sandy's rod and casts into an eddy. Sandy pokes at the fire and lifts the lid on the pot. Steam curls up, but the water isn't boiling. I listen to the creek gurgle, to Sandy and Rachel talking, to the hum of Keith's reel. Then I hear another sound, a clattering of stones, a clattering of hooves against gravel.

I stand up, expecting a moose or more caribou. But it's horses, four horses and two riders clomping towards us. They stop. The horses drop their heads and swish their tails. Guns are slung over the saddles and a man with a wide-brimmed hat leans over and stares at our overturned canoes.

The man looks at me, then at Sandy. "Whatcha all doin'?" he asks in a southern drawl. "Canoein'?"

"Yeah," agrees Sandy, "we're canoeing."

The man nods and flicks the reins. As the horses walk past I see the curl of sheep horns, several sets lashed to the load on a pack horse. What was recently grazing in a high meadow is now destined for a Big Bull Night in Texas.

June 1979 - Cathedral Mountains, B.C.

I scramble up the chimney, grabbing exposed chunks of granite, kicking steps in the heavy snow. I loop a sling over a finger of rock and wedge a chock into a crack. Tying a figure-eight knot in the rope around my waist, I clip it into the anchor carabiner, twirling the screw gate to lock it.

"On belay," I yell, but I can feel the wind pick up the words and fling them into my face, along with the mist that is streaming up the cleft.

"On belaaaay!"

"Climbing," the words from below sound thin.

"Cliiimb."

I pull the rope, sliding my hands in the approved Outward Bound belay shuffle. The rope is rough, I can feel the friction against my back. The clouds thin out for a moment, and I get a glimpse of space, a lot of space. I wonder what my students are making of this; it's exciting enough for me. My feet are cold, but I try to ignore it. I have nine students to belay before we can set up our bivouac near the summit of Mt. McKeen.

Snake River.

The rope slides up steadily. Whoever is tied in is climbing quickly. I bend over for a look and see a face framed by a toque and orange helmet.

"All right, Rachel!" I say. "You're zooming up that chimney."

At the end of the twenty-six-day course I walk with my group to the Hope-Princeton Highway. It's a hot Similkameen morning and the scent of sagebrush is heavy. Meadowlarks sit on fence posts, their gurgling songs clear and strong. A Greyhound bus pulls over and I wave good-bye to the departing students.

Rachel goes back to school in Toronto and a Canada Post friendship develops. When I move to the Yukon, she comes to visit. She works as an assistant on Yukon Outward Bound courses, and we paddle wild rivers together.

One of the problems inherent with outdoor courses is the aura that attaches itself to instructors. Because they are comfortable in the back country and proficient in high-risk activities, leaders gain a status inversely proportional to the size of their bank accounts. At the end of the first course I instructed at Outward Bound, my group sliced a dead hiking boot in half, bronzed it, and glued it to a plaque bearing the inscription "Demi-God Ken." I hoped it was a joke.

On trips with Rachel, I try to exorcise the instructor part of my personality. I hope decision making will always be a shared responsibility.

Saxifrage.

August 1986 - Snake River

Rain drips. We put our heads down and paddle. It's easy to develop a rhythm, the hours eaten up as the shore drifts upstream in the mist. It's too miserable to stop.

"I'm getting chilled," says Wendy.

Suddenly, I realize that I'm bloody cold too. The weather has insidiously sucked away our energy since we crawled out of our sleeping bags. I remember becoming hypothermic on just such a day on the Nahanni, paddling through the fog and rain, wanting to put the miles behind us. "I don't need to stop," I had said, "I'm fine."

A crosswind whips horizontal rain in my face. Sandy and Lois are somewhere downstream, out of sight. Tracee and Keith are just ahead. I look back. Graham hangs out over a broad sweep stroke and Rachel is paddling hard. They turn and nose into a side channel, hoping for a short-cut. The problem with short-cuts is that they usually turn into long-cuts . . . and you are never quite sure, when you eventually paddle back into the main channel, whether you're ahead or behind.

I hate to leave a lone boat behind. Accidents can happen without warning, while help drifts swiftly downstream. "We'd better wait for them," I say.

We eddy out beside a dark, rain-soaked log jam. I huddle in my jacket and watch water drip from the naked branches above me. Fingers of mist reach from the low clouds and grope at the tree tops.

In a while the ghostlike shape of a canoe appears in the fog. We paddle towards it.

"I know we should have stayed in the main channel," Rachel snaps. "Don't look so goddamn self-righteous." They stroke grimly past.

The flare-up is as sudden and violent as a summer thunderstorm. The words cut like an incision, the pain sharper due to their edge of truth. I had, no doubt, been wearing my best "disapproving instructor" look. Wendy doesn't say anything, and we follow their boat, already obscured by the rain.

December 1990 - Whitehorse

I reach for the next handhold. My upper body slides sideways until my weight is over my right climbing shoe. Rivulets of sweat flow into my eyes. With tight forearms and aching fingers, I let go with my right hand and stretch, but my foot slips. I land on both feet on the basement floor and look at the pieces of wood and ceramic that make up my improvised climbing wall.

"In Dawson it's minus forty-five degrees, in Mayo minus forty-six. Up in Old Crow it's clear and minus forty-three. Once again, in Whitehorse it's thirty-four below with a wind out of the north at ten kilometers an hour, creating a very high wind chill."

I walk over to the wood bin and pick up a spruce log. The voice on the radio has finally finished talking temperatures.

"In a moment, we'll have the results of the latest fur sales in Toronto."

I pull up the handle on the wood stove, lower the heavy door, and toss in the log. The coals sizzle and fingers of flame tickle the wood. Acrid smoke puffs into the basement. I turn my head away and close the door hurriedly.

I shake out my arms and dip my hands in a chalk bag. Squeezing a small chunk of hockey stick that is securely screwed into a stud, I step onto a home-fired clay foothold. I try to concentrate on the exercise, try to tune out the radio, now telling me how much a marten pelt is worth, what a wolverine skin sells for, whether there are buyers for timber wolf hides.

"Otters were offered at nineteen dollars, and the top price at this auction was twenty-four dollars. No muskrats were offered . . ."

August 1986 - Snake River

"It feels great to paddle," says Rachel.

We need to be in Fort McPherson in four days and it's hundreds of kilometers downriver. Today is the first day I've paddled with Rachel, and we both feel like using our muscles. We leave the others behind.

"Are you getting hungry yet?" she asks.

"Yeah, maybe we should find a place to cook supper."

We haven't seen the other canoes since we schooled together for a floating snack in midafternoon. The plan is to stop for supper, and then float into the twilight. It's a good time to see animals along the river banks, and a good way to put in a few more kilometers before tumbling into our sleeping bags.

"How about that gravel bar?" I ask.

She nods, we dig in our paddles, and the bow crunches on the sand.

"I hope the others aren't pissed off that we didn't stop sooner," says Rachel. "I wonder how far behind they are?"

We toss driftwood onto the rocks next to the river, where there is a patch of sand for a cooking fire. I haul the pot bag from the canoe and Rachel lights the fire. She wanders down the beach while water heats for tea. I have a quick bath in the river. Sandy and Lois paddle around the corner as I step into my pants.

Flapjacks.

"The rest aren't far behind," says Sandy, and in a few minutes the other boats pull up.

"Is tonight's supper in your boat?" I ask Wendy.

She nods and lifts a red day pack of food.

"What's that noise?" asks Rachel.

I hear squeaky cries from the river and look up from the fire. Four faces are staring towards us, three whiskered faces the size of my fist, and one twice as big. Only heads and necks are visible above the surface of the river. They look disembodied.

"Otters," says Sandy.

The otters float by, letting the current whisk them downstream. The only movement is the mother's mouth opening and closing, opening and closing, uttering shrill warning cries to her three pups.

Otters were offered at nineteen dollars . . .

August 1987 - Hess River

Graham, Rachel, Wendy, and I grunt up a game trail that winds through the willows, eventually breaking out into an alpine meadow. A herd of caribou, cows and calves, are grazing half a kilometer up the valley, between us and the col we are heading towards.

"Let's go up to the ridge," says Graham. He scrambles straight up. Before Wendy, Rachel, and I climb out of the valley on a route which will take us above the caribou, we angle closer. We want a better look.

We zigzag towards the herd for a few minutes. The nearest caribou lifts her head and splays out her forelegs. Suddenly, several dozen pairs of dark eyes are staring right at us. I stop and try to be invisible, but it's too late. They bolt up the valley and circle towards the ridge. The caribou find Graham at the crest, and gallop skittishly away.

I plod up to the col, drop my pack, and sit on it. Rachel and Wendy puff up over the rise to join me and break out a snack. We wait, and when Graham hikes down the ridge he looks pissed off.

"We blew a chance there," says Graham angrily.

"I didn't want to scare them," I say defensively.

"You walked right towards them!"

Glib retorts roll from my tongue as I try to justify my actions.

"It's okay to frighten animals, it teaches them to be wary of the next human, who might be carrying a rifle. When we travel in the bush we're a part of the natural system, and we have a right to a direct route to our destination."

Even as the words roll from my tongue and dissipate in the mountain air, I know that my excuses are lame. In the north, animals need all the time they can get for feeding. Fleeing depletes precious energy that could tip the scales between survival and starvation during the difficult winter, which even in mid-August is already on its way.

We are visitors to the wilderness, uninvited guests with more responsibilities than rights.

August 1986 - Snake River

On a ridge above the Snake, Wendy took our camera from its case and we crept up to three bull caribou resting in the lee of a boulder. She captured their rigid posture and startled eyes on Kodachrome 64. At first we were pleased with the slide — we ordered prints and glued them on home-made calendars for Christmas presents. When I last looked at the picture, I saw our own version of a Big Bull Night. We don't have a head mount, but the slide documents an impact that I now try to avoid.

Years ago, at Virginia Falls, I met a old man who had spent several seasons working on the banks of the Nahanni during the 1930s. He was gray-haired and stooped, but his eyes were young. He wanted to tell me about the days, half a century ago, when it was natural for him to look for animals down the barrel of his rifle.

"One day my partner and I shot a couple of Dall sheep ewes," he said. "One minute they were so alive, the next minute bloody white heaps on a hillside. After a while I just couldn't kill any more."

His journey back to the Nahanni was both pilgrimage and reunion. He spoke of his hunting days with candor and lack of embarrassment, telling me that the person that he used to be no longer existed. He was full of hope that if he could change, so could others.

We paddle past the mouth of the Snake into the Peel River which is brown and bloated from a summer storm. All I can see are low wooded hills. The mountains, the caribou, and the Dall sheep are already memories, and even though we're two hundred kilometers from Ft. McPherson, it feels as though the trip is over.

It isn't over, of course. What we've taken through our interaction with the land will stay with us. We take from the wilderness, but the best thing we can leave in return is nothing at all.

Big bull caribou.

HOW TO HELP PRESERVE THE TATSHENSHINI

Tatshenshini Wild is spearheading the international campaign to preserve the Tatshenshini and Alsek Wilderness. If you want to become informed about the latest developments in the struggle to save the Tatshenshini, write to Tatshenshini Wild, 843-810 West Broadway, Vancouver, B.C., Canada, V5Z 4C9. If you wish to help protect "North America's wildest river" with a tax-deductible donation, mail it to the same address.

The only way that government officials will understand the strength of public feeling about preserving the Tatshenshini is for a flood of letters to wash up on their desks. They need to realize that the wilderness values of this area far outweigh the short-term economic benefits of the Windy Craggy Mine ... a mine with many associated environmental risks.

In Canada, write to The Premier of British Columbia, Legislative Buildings, Victoria, B.C., V8V 1X4 and to The Minister of Environment, House of Commons, Ottawa, Ontario, K1A 0A6.

In the United States, write to your local Congressperson and to the Governor of Alaska, P.O. Box "A", Juneau, Alaska, 99811. We suggest that you request that a complete and comprehensive Environmental Impact Statement be done on the whole project.

The profits from the sale of this book will be used by the Western Canada Wilderness Committee for research and education on the preservation of the Tatshenshini watershed.

The Tatshenshini River.

ABOUT WESTERN CANADA WILDERNESS COMMITTEE

Western Canada Wilderness Committee is a British Columbia-based society dedicated to preserving wilderness through education and research. Started in 1980 by a handful of people, it now has 34,000 members and four branches. WCWC was instrumental in establishing the South Moresby National Park Reserve on the Queen Charlotte Islands and Carmanah Pacific Provincial Park on Vancouver Island. Protecting the Tatshenshini is currently one of its major campaigns.

Ken Madsen on the Tatshenshini River.

ABOUT THE AUTHOR

Ken Madsen is a writer, photographer, and outdoor educator living in Whitehorse, Yukon. He co-authored *Rivers of the Yukon — A Paddling Guide*, and his articles and photos have appeared in *Explore*, *Paddler*, *River Runner*, *Currents*, and *Canoe* magazines. He has paddled throughout western North America, Mexico, and New Zealand, including many "first descents" in Yukon, northern B.C., and Alaska. When he isn't exploring wilderness rivers, he is working for wilderness preservation as the president of the Whitehorse-based society, Friends of Yukon Rivers.